DAIRY-FREE
Delicious

DAIRY-FREE
Delicious

KATY SALTER

PHOTOGRAPHY BY LAURA EDWARDS

The Countryman Press

A division of W. W. Norton & Company

Independent Publishers Since 1923

For Mom and Dad, for everything.

First American Edition 2016

First published in 2015 by
Quadrille Publishing Limited
www.quadrille.co.uk

PUBLISHING DIRECTOR: Jane O'Shea
CREATIVE DIRECTOR: Helen Lewis
SENIOR EDITOR: Céline Hughes
DESIGN: Katherine Keeble
PHOTOGRAPHY: Laura Edwards
FOOD STYLIST: Emily Jonzen
PROPS STYLIST: Tabitha Hawkins
PRODUCTION: Vincent Smith, Sasha Hawkes

The Countryman Press
www.countrymanpress.com

A division of W. W. Norton & Company, Inc.
500 Fifth Avenue, New York, NY 10110
www.wwnorton.com

ISBN 978-1-58157-351-0 (hardcover)

10 9 8 7 6 5 4 3 2 1

Library of Congress Cataloging-in-Publication Data
Salter, Katy, author.
    Dairy-free delicious / Katy Salter ; photography
by Laura Edwards. --
First American edition.
        pages cm
    Includes index.
    "Independent publishers since 1923."
1. Milk-free diet--Recipes. 2. Dairy substitutes. 3.
Lactose intolerance.
    I. Edwards, Laura, photographer. II. Title.
    RM234.5.S35 2016
    641.5'63--dc23
                                    2015030751

INTRODUCTION

MY STORY

Lactose intolerance was not in the plan. My three great loves as a child were reading, writing, and eating. As an adult, I have been lucky enough to combine the latter two and make a living out of them. I became a journalist and eventually landed my dream job as features editor of a food magazine.

The unofficial job description of a food writer is to "go everywhere; eat everything," and for several years I did just that—trying everything from Croatian truffle ice cream to Kenyan crocodile. The ability to eat weird and wonderful foods was something I took for granted.

Then food poisoning struck. A few bouts of gastroenteritis followed. My once-Teflon stomach was now weak, and I would often be sick for no obvious reason. Unexplained and extremely painful stomach cramps meant I was regularly out sick from work, and, when I wasn't, I felt permanently exhausted. It seems obvious in retrospect, but at the time I didn't make the connection to my diet. I spent half of 2011 at the doctor's having blood tests for various conditions—everything (blessedly) came back negative.

Eventually, I was told to try two elimination diets and keep a food diary. The first two weeks were spent cutting out gluten, which made no difference —the cramps and nausea were as bad as ever. The second test was a dairy elimination diet—no butter, no yogurt, no cheese, and certainly no milk. The changes were instant and profound. No more stomach cramps, no more nausea, and my energy started to return—no more feeling like a retiree shuffling around pretending to be a 30-year-old. The dairy had to go. Sure, I'd miss flat whites, Parmesan, and chocolate buttons (especially the chocolate buttons), but I was so happy not to be in pain that it didn't seem like a sacrifice.

The biggest difficulty has been the incompatibility of living dairy-free and eating out. After all, this was not just about my diet, food is also my livelihood. Things I took for granted were now tricky: grabbing a pizza with friends, reviewing a French restaurant (all that butter), going to weddings. I reluctantly became that fussy eater who asks for the dressing on the side. It made me realize how intolerant our food culture is of people with dietary requirements —be it people with intolerances, allergies, celiac disease, vegetarians, vegans, or those who don't eat certain foods for health or religious reasons. Just because you can't eat everything, it doesn't mean you don't love good food. Everyone should feel comfortable and welcome when they eat out.

Sure, there have been times when I've fallen off the wagon a little ... and felt the consequences. I lived in New York for part of 2012 and discovered the "miracle cure" of lactase tablets from the drugstore—little supplements that help your body break down lactose. They helped for a while but after doubling up in pain on the sidewalk after eating a cheeseburger, I realized that living dairy-free was permanent for me, something that couldn't be solved by popping a pill. I chose not just to accept it but embrace it, and started creating dairy-free recipes to help people in the same position.

There is no cheeseburger so delicious it's worth crying over. Especially not when, with a few tweaks to your diet, you can live dairy-free and enjoy food every bit as delicious as the pizzas, ice creams, chocolates, and cheeses you used to eat. There are so many people out there who have problems digesting dairy. Many are people who live to eat, to cook, and to entertain just as much as I do. If you're one of them, I hope you find plenty of recipes in this book to reignite your love affair with good food.

WHAT IS LACTOSE INTOLERANCE?

Lactose is a type of sugar found in milk. It can't be absorbed by the body as it is, so when you eat anything containing lactose, the lactase in your digestive system gets to work breaking down the lactose into other simple sugars that can be absorbed into your body. Lactase is an enzyme produced by the body to break down lactose.

The problem is lots of us don't have enough lactase in our systems to break down lactose efficiently. This is where the sexy symptoms start: bloating, stomach cramps and pains, diarrhea, flatulence, and nausea. None of them are life-threatening, but they can seriously impact your quality of life.

Lactose intolerance is exceedingly common. The figures vary, but studies suggest that, for example, 15 percent of the British population is lactose intolerant. That's 9.5 million people. Worldwide, it's estimated that some 65 percent of adults have some level of difficulty digesting lactose.

Lactose intolerance is particularly prevalent in certain ethnic groups, including people of East Asian, West African, Jewish, and Arabic descent. It's believed that primary lactase deficiency, which is inherited, is particularly common in ethnic groups that have a shorter history of including milk as a key part of their diet.

Lactose intolerance can also occur at any stage in life. This is called secondary lactase deficiency. Babies and young children can be sensitive to dairy but often grow out of it. Both adults and children can develop lactose intolerance after gastroenteritis, after long courses of antibiotics, as a result of chemotherapy, or as a symptom of other conditions, including celiac and Crohn's disease. For some people, secondary lactase deficiency may be temporary, but for others, it can be permanent. Either way, our bodies naturally produce less lactase as we age, so adjusting to a diet with less or no dairy in it can be helpful to many.

The severity of lactose intolerance varies from person to person. I can't handle any cow's milk products, including milk chocolate, without getting stomach cramps. But I do eat a little bit of sheep yogurt and goat and sheep cheese in small quantities. Cow's milk typically contains more lactose than that from other dairy animals like goats, sheep, and buffalo. I also sometimes drink lactose-free milk, where all the lactose is removed by a special process.

If you think you might be lactose intolerant, it is always advisable to speak to your doctor first and keep a food and symptoms diary. They may suggest an elimination diet or in some instances, further blood sugar or other tests that can diagnose lactose intolerance.

WHAT IS A MILK ALLERGY?

Cow's milk allergy is an immune-system response to one or more of the proteins in cow's milk (most commonly casein). This type of allergy is called an IgE-mediated milk allergy. When people with the allergy consume milk, the body goes into red alert, mistakenly producing antibodies to fight off what it perceives as a threat. The symptoms come on quickly and can include a rash or hives, eczema, wheezing and coughing, swollen lips, vomiting, and stomach pain. In rare cases, it can cause anaphylaxis, which needs immediate emergency treatment.

There is also another type of cow's milk allergy, called a non-IgE-mediated cow's milk protein allergy. It was formerly called a milk protein intolerance, but it can be classified as an allergy. It is more common in children, and symptoms include eczema, vomiting, stomach cramps, and diarrhea, but not hives or wheezing/breathing problems. The symptoms can take longer to develop than with an IgE-mediated allergy, and can often develop a few hours after consuming milk products.

Milk allergies are more common in children than adults. They affect around two-five percent of babies and young children, and usually start in infancy. Luckily, many children with a milk allergy grow out of it and only 0.1 percent of people over the age of five have one.

If you suspect that you or your child has a milk allergy, you should always consult your doctor.

LEARNING TO READ THE LABELS

It's easy to cut milk and cheese out of your diet, but what about all those products that contain milk? Dairy shows up in an astonishing array of foodstuffs, from some breads and chips to salad dressings, and even some wines (I like to think this last one explains some terrible "miscarriage of justice" hangovers I've had after two glasses of Sauvignon). Always check the label and look out for terms like the following:
* Buttermilk
* Casein
* Caseinates
* Ghee
* Milk protein
* Milk powder
* Milk solids
* Skim milk powder
* Whey

THE IMPLICATIONS OF CUTTING OUT DAIRY

If you're cutting out dairy, then it's important to ensure you're getting all the nutrients you would from milk, cheese, and yogurt elsewhere in your diet.

Dairy products are a good source of calcium, important for building strong teeth and bones when you're young, and keeping them strong in later life, which can help prevent osteoporosis and regulate your muscles and heartbeat.

Look for dairy-free milks such as soy, almond, and oat milk, which have been fortified with calcium. If you are lactose intolerant, rather than allergic

to milk, you could also try lactose-free milk, which uses a special process to remove all the lactose from milk. For babies with a milk allergy, consult your doctor who can advise on the most suitable type of formula.

There are many other good dietary sources of calcium and you will find many recipes using them in this book. Include the following in your diet wherever possible:
* Dark leafy greens like kale, broccoli, and watercress
* Most nuts, including almonds, Brazil nuts, and hazelnuts
* Tofu
* Beans
* Sesame seeds
* Salmon
* Sardines
* Soybeans
* Whole grains, including whole-grain bread

Adults need 700 mg of calcium a day, preferably from your diet, and a balanced dairy-free diet that includes nondairy milks and the foods above should do this. If you're concerned about the amount of calcium in your diet, talk to your doctor before taking supplements, as supplements in high doses can be harmful.

Our bodies also need vitamin D to absorb calcium. We get most of this from sunlight, but if you live in a rainy land like Britain, it's also a good idea to include the following in your diet, which are all good sources of vitamin D:
* Eggs
* Fortified cereals
* Oily fish

SO WHAT CAN YOU EAT INSTEAD OF DAIRY?

The good news is, there are lots of delicious dairy alternatives you can eat—and the situation is improving all the time. My local café now does an almond-milk flat white and some grocery stores now stock coconut yogurt. Both were unthinkable even a few years ago.

One important thing to note is that you don't need to panic-buy lots of processed and expensive free-from products that are stuffed with weird, unpronounceable ingredients. There are lots of free-from cookies, cakes, and snacks on the market but I hope this book shows that it's really easy to make your own. In many cases it will be cheaper, and it will give you more control over what you and your family are eating. I've tried to stick to natural ingredients in this book wherever possible, and certainly to avoid anything with glucose-fructose/high-fructose corn syrup in it.

Nut, rice, coconut, oat, and soy milk are now available in convenience and grocery stores, and will form a key part of your dairy-free diet. Look for ones from non-GMO and sustainable sources when appropriate. It's also easy to make your own nut, oat, and rice milks, which have the added benefit of being free from any emulsifiers and stabilizers. There are recipes for all of these on pages 40–41 in the breakfast chapter, and a recipe for Mexican-style horchata in the dessert chapter (see page 154). A cool glass of horchata on a hot day is every bit as irresistible as a glass of milk.

There is still lingering confusion over eggs and whether or not they are dairy. Eggs are not dairy. Assuming you are not vegan or allergic to eggs, then enjoy at your will—I use them in many recipes in this book (free-range, naturally).

Meat, fish, beans, nuts, and all fruits and vegetables are all naturally dairy free. So are animal fats such as duck and goose fat (for delicious roasties or the duck confit on page 75) and lard (which makes delicious savory pie dough). Oils such as olive and canola can often be used instead of butter in cooking and in cakes (for more on this see pages 12–13).

For a full list of useful ingredients to include in your diet, turn to the pantry section on pages 10–13.

HOW THIS BOOK WORKS
All the recipes in this book are 100 percent dairy free. The book is specifically aimed at people who can't or won't eat dairy, rather than a generalist free-from book, but I have tried to include a decent number of options for those with other dietary restrictions. Equally, most of the recipes using

almond milk can be made with soy milk and vice versa if you cannot ingest one or the other. The recipes in this book can broadly be divided into two types.

The first are those recipes based on dishes or ingredients from countries where dairy forms a very minimal part of the diet. Good examples of these include the creamy Vietnamese curry on page 82 or the Khao soi noodles inspired by a Thai street food dish on page 66. As a side note, when eating out I find Vietnamese, Thai, and Japanese restaurants among the best bets for dairy-free dining. French and Italian are probably the trickiest.

The second type of recipes are those that would normally be made with dairy. No one should have to live without pizza, ice cream, chocolate birthday cake, or lasagna, so I have devised dairy-free alternatives. Most of the classic dairy dishes are here—from eggs Benedict with a silky hollandaise (see page 22) to a Victoria sandwich filled with vanilla whipped coconut cream (see page 147). There's no fondue, but I think we'll just have to learn to live without cauldrons of melted cheese. Otherwise, with a little determination and adjustment (some dairy-free alternatives don't behave quite as milk or cream would), I believe most dishes can be made *Dairy-Free Delicious*.

A FEW NOTES ON THE RECIPES
* All eggs are extra-large unless otherwise stated
* All lemons are unwaxed
* All almond and soy milk is unsweetened
* All coconut milk is the whole kind
* All mayonnaise is the whole kind
* Always check the label as some free-from products contain glucose-fructose/high-fructose corn syrup—I have tried to avoid using such products in all the book's recipes

THE DAIRY-FREE PANTRY

Stock your refrigerator and pantry with these versatile ingredients and you'll always be ready to make a wealth of dairy-free meals and desserts.

ALMONDS

Almonds are a rich source of calcium, so sprinkle flaked ones on your cereal or Bircher muesli in the mornings, and keep a bag of whole almonds on hand to snack on at work. I use toasted, slivered almonds in baking and breakfast recipes, and as an alternative to Parmesan to top salads, such as the classic Caesar on page 46.

ALMOND MILK

An incredibly useful and versatile dairy-free ingredient. Not only does unsweetened almond milk contain calcium and taste pleasant in tea and on cereal, its subtle, neutral flavor means it works well as a baking ingredient and substitute for cow's milk. You can also mix almond milk with a little lemon juice as an alternative to buttermilk. Look for brands made with non-GMO ingredients, fortified with vitamins like B12 and E, and always without sugar (all the recipes using almond milk in this book are made with unsweetened almond milk). Commercial nut milks are emulsified so they can sometimes separate when added straight to the pan during cooking. For savory dishes, such as the Dauphinoise potatoes on page 77, you can make a basic white sauce to avoid this happening.

AVOCADOS

Avocados are sometimes known as "butter pears," which is a perfect description of the creamy flesh hidden inside that scaly, fat-bottomed exterior. Avocados are packed with nutrients like vitamin E, iron, and potassium and are a useful dairy-free ingredient—use them to make chocolate mousse or spread on toast for breakfast.

BAKING MARGARINE

Use baking margarine to make flaky pastries, airy sponge cakes, and short cookies. It may not match the delights of real butter when it comes to taste, but it's a good substitute for unsalted butter in baking as it has a similar consistency. Depending on the recipe, I often use a little vanilla extract or cinnamon to enhance the flavor of the cake or cookie and to make up for the lack of that creamy, real-butter taste. People can never tell the difference! Look for brands made with sustainable palm oil and without trans fats. Be careful to avoid the spreadable kinds, however, as they contain buttermilk.

CACAO NIBS

Cacao nibs are little roasted chips of the cacao bean. They are usually ground into a paste to make chocolate, but are increasingly popular as a food in their own right (find them in health food stores). The first time you try cacao nibs can be disconcerting, especially if you're used to sweet milk chocolate. They have an intense, earthy flavor—chocolatey but not sweet. After you've gotten used to them, they're very delectable—which is good news as cacao is packed with antioxidants and minerals, including magnesium. Eat a handful as a snack, sprinkle onto cereal and oatmeal, or use in the cacao nib and cranberry granola or espresso and raw chocolate granita recipes (see pages 28 and 122 respectively).

CASHEW NUTS

Creamy, biscuity cashews have a multitude of uses in a dairy-free diet. Make delicious cashew milk to drink or pour over cereal, spread cashew butter on toast, make cashew cream to serve with desserts (the recipe for macadamia cream on page 34 can also be made with the same weight of cashews), or use instead of cheese in savory dishes like curries, stir-fries, and pesto. Not only do cashews taste delicious, they're also a great source of magnesium and zinc.

UNSWEETENED COCOA POWDER

A dairy-free diet doesn't mean you have to give up your favorite chocolate desserts. Good quality 70 percent cocoa doesn't contain cow's milk so you can use it in cakes and desserts, and to make hot chocolate. If you're lactose-intolerant then most brands should be okay to use—they don't contain any milk in the product but will have a warning on the label saying they "may contain milk traces" because they're produced in factories that may also produce milk chocolates. If you have a dairy allergy or want to make certain there are no traces, look for dairy-free or vegan brands that are guaranteed free from traces of milk.

COCONUT CREAM

Thick, luscious coconut cream is the best substitute for heavy or clotted cream. It has a mild flavor that goes well with vanilla and, if you chill it in the refrigerator first, it whisks up into fluffy clouds of whipped coconut cream. All brands are not created equal, so find one with a pleasant taste that thickens up well when chilled.

COCONUT MILK

People sometimes tell me they "hate" coconut, but this mild and creamy milk doesn't have the overpowering taste of dry unsweetened coconut—it's subtle and incredibly useful in dairy-free cooking, so I urge you to give it a try. Coconut milk forms the base of incredible ice creams and a wealth of classic curries and noodle dishes from India and southeast Asia, and it's pretty much one of the most versatile ingredients you can keep in your pantry. Please note all the recipes using coconut milk in this book are made with whole coconut milk—dishes like the ice cream and custard just won't work with the watery, reduced-fat stuff. Try a few brands until you find one you like—again, I like one that always has a delicious, thick layer of coconut cream at the top of the can, much like gold-top milk.

COCONUT OIL

Yes, more coconut! Heart-healthy coconut oil comes from the meaty coconut flesh and is solid at room temperature but melts with a little gentle heating. Look for extra-virgin raw coconut oil and use it to make homemade granola or flapjacks, or for frying and roasting vegetables, such as the caramelized Chantenay carrots on page 105.

COCONUT YOGURT

Warning: coconut yogurt is addictive. Luckily it's good for you—a vegan yogurt with probiotic cultures made from coconut milk. It has a creamy taste with a slightly sour tang—similar to Greek yogurt, and a voluptuous, thick consistency. Find it in some larger grocery stores or health food stores.

DAIRY-FREE SUNFLOWER SPREAD

I won't lie to you—there's no free-from spread that can compare to the taste of salted butter on a crusty baguette. But for cooking and baking, dairy-free sunflower spread is incredibly versatile. I like a vegan dairy-free spread, which is spreadable straight from the refrigerator, but whichever brand you go for, check that it's free from trans fats. Always read the label because some sunflower spreads contain buttermilk.

SEMISWEET CHOCOLATE

A key ingredient in many of the cakes and desserts in this book is 70-percent-cocoa-solids semisweet chocolate. Always check the label—good-quality brands don't contain any milk products, but some cheaper or flavored ones can. As with the cocoa powder, dark chocolate sometimes comes with a "may contain milk traces" warning depending on the factory where it was made, so if you have a dairy allergy, look for specialist dairy-free brands.

DARK LEAFY GREENS

Green leafy vegetables like kale, watercress, and broccoli are an excellent source of calcium, among many other nutrients, so make a daily get-your-greens juice in the morning (see page 16), or add these veggies to dishes whenever you can.

MAYONNAISE

I've been asked lots of times if mayonnaise contains dairy. The short answer is—it shouldn't. Good-quality, whole mayonnaise is made with eggs and oil, like mayonnaise should be. It's the reduced-fat brands that often add milk products, so always check the label or, if in doubt, make your own.

MUSTARD POWDER

Mustard powder is what I call a "disguiser." I use a little to mask the taste of oat cream or sunflower spread in a savory sauce and to ape the savory bite of sharp Cheddar or Parmesan. You'll find spices like nutmeg and cinnamon, and lots of vanilla used in this book's sweet recipes for the same reason. Keeping a well-stocked spice drawer pays dividends for the dairy-free cook.

OAT CREAM

Oat cream is made by emulsifying oats with oil. In terms of color and consistency, it is a good alternative to light cream in baking. I don't tend to pour it on desserts because there's no getting around the earthy taste (make cashew or macadamia cream, or a batch of whipped coconut cream for this purpose instead). It does have a tendency to split when heated, so for many savory recipes I find it works better when added to a béchamel or simple white sauce instead, with a little mustard powder (see above).

OLIVE OIL

Light olive oil makes incredible cakes—fluffy sponges and moist chocolate numbers. It's not a straightforward case of swapping the same volume of oil for the weight of butter, so stick to the volume specified in the recipes.

PANKO

Panko is a crispy and very dry Japanese bread crumb. It adds color, crunch, and texture to the top of savory dishes like lasagna, which would normally be topped with cheese.

RICE MILK

Rice milk is one of the most pleasant dairy-free milks to drink on its own, especially when flavored with vanilla. It's also easy to make your own (see page 40). However, I don't tend to use it much in cooking as it is quite thin and watery compared to the more robust almond and soy milks. It's also important to note that rice milk in the UK is not recommended for children under five years old because it contains low levels of inorganic arsenic.

SESAME SEEDS

Another excellent source of calcium, so get to sprinkling sesame seeds on yogurt, salads, curries, and a million other dishes.

SOY MILK AND YOGURT

There are lots of conflicting studies on the health benefits, or otherwise, of soy milk. For those who can't eat nuts as well as dairy, it can be a very useful alternative, so I have included it in this book, albeit sparingly as I'm not a huge fan of the taste. Look for brands fortified with calcium. All the recipes using soy milk in this book use the unsweetened version. Many of the recipes using almond milk can also be made using soy if you prefer.

TOFU

Tofu is a good source of calcium. It also takes on strong flavors easily, so it's a brilliant addition to curries, Thai, and Vietnamese dishes.

VANILLA

You'll find I've used vanilla extract in many of the book's sweet recipes, as its comforting aroma subtly masks free-from products such as sunflower spread. Use a good-quality real vanilla extract (rather than the cheaper vanillin). I'm also a big fan of real vanilla powder—a tiny pinch is a quick alternative to scraping the seeds from a vanilla bean.

VEGAN CREAM CHEESE

Vegan cream cheese is usually made from tofu. I wouldn't eat it plain or smear it on a bagel as it has—shall we say—an acquired taste, but it whips up with confectioners' sugar and lemon or vanilla into a delicious, fluffy frosting for cakes.

VEGETABLE, PEANUT, CANOLA, OR SUNFLOWER OIL

These neutral cooking oils are used throughout the book, and not just for savory dishes—they also make light and delicious cakes.

VEGETABLE SHORTENING

Vegetable shortening is a solid fat that makes perfect crumbly pastries. Look for brands that don't contain trans fats and that use palm oil from sustainable sources.

BREAKFAST

ICED MOCHA

1 tablespoon unsweetened cocoa
1½ tablespoons maple syrup
1 teaspoon vanilla extract
1 shot of freshly brewed espresso
1 cup vanilla soy or rice milk,
    chilled
Ice cubes

Serves 1

Wish you could drink those coffee shop mochas that come laced with milk and chocolate syrup? Make your own at home with your favorite dairy-free milk and a jolt of espresso to kick-start the morning.

Put the cocoa, maple syrup, and vanilla in a mixing pitcher. Pour in the hot espresso and whisk to combine. Let cool.

Once cool, pour in the soy or rice milk and whisk again. Add a few ice cubes to a highball glass. Pour over the mocha mixture and enjoy.

GET-YOUR-GREENS JUICE

1¾ ounces baby leaf spinach
1 ounce watercress
3½ ounces cucumber, cut into
    chunks
2 eating apples, cored and cut
    into chunks
Large handful of mint
Juice of ½ lime

Serves 1

Delicious, nutritious leafy vegetables: we all know we should be eating more of them. Green juice is an easy way to sneak some breakfast veg into your diet, and here's my take. Packed with spinach, watercress, and cucumber, with added apple for sweetness (because no one wants to down a pint of pure watercress).

Add all the ingredients to your juicer according to the directions. Stir the juice once and pour into a glass. Feel virtuous.

BANANA AND RASPBERRY SHAKE

1 very ripe banana, frozen whole
    in its skin
Scant ⅔ cup raspberries
¼ cup rolled oats
½ teaspoon ground nutmeg
2 teaspoons honey
⅔ cup almond or vanilla
    rice milk

Serves 1

Bruised and blackened bananas never get thrown away in our house. They go into the freezer, whole, waiting to do service in banana breads, muffins, and in quick and filling breakfast shakes like this one. Using a frozen banana keeps smoothies and shakes cold and gives them a lovely thick texture that isn't watered down by ice.

Take the banana out of the freezer half an hour before you want to use it. Alternatively, defrost it in the microwave for 10 to 20 seconds. The idea is to soften it just enough so you can peel the skin off.

Put the peeled banana, raspberries, and oats into a blender. Add the nutmeg, honey, and almond or rice milk and blitz for 20 seconds, until smooth. Pour into a tall glass, add a straw, and drink immediately.

CLASSIC PANCAKES

Scant 1 cup all-purpose flour
Pinch of sea salt
2 medium eggs
1 ½ cups almond, soy, or rice milk
Vegetable oil, for frying

Makes 8 to 10

Thin pancakes, or crêpes, can easily be made dairy free, using your favorite dairy-free milk (I normally use almond). Top with classic lemon and sugar, sliced banana and maple syrup, summer berries and whipped coconut cream (see page 137), or apple compote, toasted pecans, and a dollop of coconut yogurt.

Sift the flour into a large, lipped bowl and add the salt. Whisk together the eggs and almond, soy, or rice milk in a separate pitcher or bowl. Make a well in the center of the flour and pour in the egg mixture. Whisk together briskly until you have a smooth batter. Let stand for 10 minutes.

Preheat the oven to its lowest setting and place a plate in the middle of the oven.

Heat a small nonstick skillet over medium-high heat. Add a few drops of oil, then use a piece of paper towel to spread this all over the bottom of the pan until you have a light mist of oil covering the surface (you might want to briefly remove the pan from the heat to do this). Turn the heat up to high.

Pour approximately 2 tablespoons of batter into the pan (just enough to cover the bottom). Swirl the batter around until you've covered the bottom of the pan and there's no liquid batter left. Once the edges of the pancake start to come away from the pan, use a wide spatula to loosen the pancake and flip it over. Cook for another 20 to 30 seconds, until both sides are golden and lacy.

Place each pancake on the warmed plate as soon as it is cooked and return to the warmed oven, layering a piece of paper towel between each pancake to prevent them from sticking together. Repeat with the remaining batter to cook the rest, adding a little more oil to the pan every couple of pancakes, if necessary.

Once the last pancake is cooked, remove the stack of pancakes from the oven and serve immediately.

SPELT "BUTTERMILK" PANCAKES WITH BACON, AVOCADO, AND MAPLE SYRUP

1 tablespoon lemon juice
1 ¼ cups almond milk
Scant 1 cup whole-grain
   spelt flour
Scant 1 ¼ cups self-rising flour
½ teaspoon baking soda
Generous pinch of sea salt
2 eggs
2 tablespoons dairy-free
   sunflower spread,
   melted and cooled
Sunflower or vegetable oil,
   for frying

TO SERVE
8 slices of lean bacon
2 avocados, sliced
Maple syrup, to drizzle

Serves 4

No one should have to live without pancakes and luckily you don't have to—there are lots of dairy-free substitutes to use in your batter. For a start, you can recreate the slightly sour tang of buttermilk by adding lemon juice to almond milk. Use this "buttermilk" to make classic American pancakes, with just a hint of worthiness (hello, whole-grain spelt flour). Stack 'em high and drizzle with maple syrup. (See photograph on page 14.)

Add the lemon juice to the almond milk, stir, and let rest for 5 minutes. Meanwhile, sift both flours into a large bowl. Fold in the baking soda and salt, using a large metal spoon. Form a well in the center.

Whisk the eggs and almond milk mixture together. Pour into the well a little at a time, whisking as you go to incorporate. When you've added about half, add the melted sunflower spread and whisk to combine. Add the rest of the almond milk and keep whisking until you have a thick, smooth batter. Let the mixture rest for 10 minutes and preheat the oven to its lowest setting.

Heat a nonstick skillet over medium-high heat. Before it gets too hot, drizzle a little oil into the pan and use paper towel to evenly grease the bottom and remove the excess. Once the pan has heated up, ladle 3 tablespoons of the batter into the pan per pancake and swirl into a circle. You will be able to fit about 2 pancakes into your pan at one time. Cook for 2 to 3 minutes, until bubbles start to form on the surface and the edges start to lift away from the pan. Flip over using a spatula and cook for 1 to 2 minutes on the other side, until golden and cooked through.

Repeat in batches until you've used up all the batter (you may need to add a little more oil after every couple of pancakes) and keep the pancakes warm on a plate in the oven on its lowest setting, layering each with a sheet of paper towel.

Meanwhile, heat a separate skillet over medium-high heat and fry the bacon until it reaches your preferred state of crispiness.

Once all the pancakes are cooked, divide them into stacks between four plates. Top with the crispy bacon, drizzle maple syrup over the top, and serve with the avocado.

BAKED EGGS WITH WILTED SPINACH, PROSCIUTTO, AND TRUFFLE OIL

7 ounces baby leaf spinach
4 slices prosciutto
8 large eggs
A few drops of truffle oil
4 large slices sourdough bread
Dairy-free sunflower spread
Sea salt and freshly ground
    black pepper

8 ramekin dishes, greased with
    vegetable oil

Serves 4

Baked eggs are a brunch staple. They're perfect for mornings when your coordination is AWOL after a few drinks the night before, as there's none of the timing, whisking, juggling fandango of eggs Benedict, but all of the deliciousness. The eggs will be ready in the time it takes you to toast some sourdough and make a strong pot of coffee.

Preheat the oven to 350 °F.

Wash the spinach, remove any tough stalks, and put into a large saucepan. Just cover with water and simmer for about 3 minutes until wilted. Drain and pat dry with paper towels, squeezing to remove any excess water.

Place a little spinach in the bottom of each greased ramekin. Tear each slice of prosciutto in two, then place one piece in the bottom of each ramekin with the spinach. Sprinkle a little salt and pepper on top.

Break an egg into each ramekin. Add a drop or two of truffle oil to each dish and an extra grind of pepper on top. Place the ramekins in a roasting pan and then pour boiling water into the pan to come about halfway up the ramekins (this water bath will prevent the eggs from drying out). Bake in the oven for 10 to 12 minutes until the eggs are just set but the yolks are still wobbly.

Meanwhile, toast the sourdough bread, butter with your favorite dairy-free spread, and cut into toast strips to dunk into the eggs. Serve two ramekins per person, along with some toast strips.

EGGS BENEDICT

2 English muffins, split in half
4 eggs
4 slices good-quality ham,
   such as Yorkshire

**FOR THE SORT-OF
HOLLANDAISE**
2 egg yolks
1 tablespoon white wine vinegar
½ cup dairy-free sunflower
   spread, melted
1 teaspoon lemon juice
Small bunch of tarragon, leaves
   only, minced
Sea salt and freshly ground
   black pepper

Serves 2

Brunch is a minefield for the dairy-free. Everything on the menu sounds delicious, but the granola is smothered in yogurt, the pancakes are full of milk, and as for the eggs Benedict—there's a lake of clarified butter in the hollandaise. I was initially nervous about making this butterific dish dairy free, but was delighted with the results I got with sunflower spread. It tastes absolutely as good as the real thing …

For the sort-of hollandaise, place a heatproof bowl over a pan of gently simmering water set over low heat, making sure the bowl doesn't touch the water. Add the egg yolks and vinegar to the bowl and whisk constantly until thickened. Slowly pour in the melted spread, whisking continuously. If the sauce looks like it's about to curdle, remove the bowl from the heat for a minute and keep whisking before returning to the pan. When the sauce is thickened and glossy, remove from the heat, whisk in the lemon juice, and season to taste. Whisk in the tarragon leaves and cover with a dish towel to keep warm.

Meanwhile, toast the muffin halves (it definitely helps to put your breakfasting companion to work here—that way they can assemble the rest of the dish while you stand guard whisking the hollandaise) and poach the eggs (see page 32).

Place two toasted muffin halves on each plate. Spread a little hollandaise on each, then top with a folded slice of the ham, then a poached egg. Drizzle the hollandaise on top and serve.

FOUR BUTTER-FREE THINGS ON TOAST

1. AVOCADO AND SMOKED SALMON ON RYE

1 ripe avocado
1 teaspoon extra-virgin olive oil
1-2 slices good rye bread per
　person
4 slices smoked salmon
Squeeze of lemon juice
Sea salt and freshly ground
　black pepper

Serves 2

Ten years ago, avocado on toast was a fringe notion–now it's every savvy breakfast and bruncher's topping of choice. Creamy avocado mashed with good olive oil and topped with delicate slivers of smoked salmon is a delicious and protein-packed way to start your day.

Slice the avocado in half, remove the pit, and scoop the flesh into a small bowl. Pour in the oil and mash with the back of a fork until all the large lumps are broken up. Add salt and pepper to taste.

Toast the rye bread and spread with the mashed avocado. Fold the slices of smoked salmon on top. Squeeze a little lemon juice on top of the salmon and finish with an extra grind of black pepper.

2. CASHEW BUTTER, BANANA, AND HONEY ON WHOLE GRAIN

This is less a recipe, more a recommendation for a delicious combination for topping thick slices of lightly toasted whole-grain toast. Calcium-packed cashew butter has a mild, distinct flavor that is very different than peanut butter. Top with slices of banana and a drizzle of honey. Sprinkle a few sesame seeds on top for an extra calcium boost.

3. HOMEMADE CHOCOLATE-AND-HAZELNUT SPREAD, AKA "NOTELLA"

1 ⅓ cups blanched hazelnuts
3 ½ ounces semisweet chocolate
⅔ cup coconut cream, plus
    extra to taste
½ teaspoon vanilla extract
1 tablespoon maple syrup
Pinch of sea salt
3 tablespoons sunflower oil

Makes 1 small jar

Whether you like it spread on toast, smeared on top of waffles, or hidden inside a crêpe, chocolate-and-hazelnut spread (its Italian name is *gianduja*) is irresistible stuff. This homemade version is more intense than the bought stuff as it's made with semisweet chocolate; stir a little extra coconut cream in at the end if you want a milkier taste.

Toast the hazelnuts in a small, dry skillet over medium-high heat until they start to turn golden and release their toasty hazelnut aroma. Keep a careful eye on them as they can burn quickly. Tip onto a plate and let cool.

Finely chop the chocolate and place in a large, lipped bowl.

Heat the coconut cream in a small saucepan over medium-high heat. Remove from the heat just before it starts to boil—when you start to see bubbles form around the edges.

Pour the cream over the chocolate and stir gently with a wooden spoon until all the chocolate has melted and you have a smooth ganache. (If there is still a little chocolate that hasn't melted, then fill the empty saucepan with water and bring to a simmer. Set the glass mixing bowl above the saucepan so it isn't touching the water and melt the last of the chocolate, stirring gently.) Add the vanilla and maple syrup and stir again until combined.

Blitz the toasted hazelnuts in a food processor until they break down first into ground nuts. Add the salt and blitz again. Keep scraping down the sides of the food processor with a spatula. Slowly trickle in the oil with the motor running, then keep going until you have a thick liquid consistency, similar to peanut butter—this will take 3 to 4 minutes. Depending on the strength of your food processor, you may not be able to break the nuts down entirely, but don't worry, it will still taste delicious.

Stir the nut mixture into the ganache and let cool completely. Stir in an extra tablespoon or two of coconut cream if you would like it a little milkier.

Spoon into an airtight, sterilized jar. It will keep in the refrigerator for several weeks, should you be able to resist snarfing it all in one go.

4. HOMEMADE BAKED BEANS

2 tablespoons olive oil
1 onion, finely diced
1 garlic clove, crushed
14-ounce can chopped tomatoes
1 tablespoon dark brown sugar
1 tablespoon blackstrap molasses
2 teaspoons English mustard
1 tablespoon cider vinegar
14-ounce can haricot beans,
    rinsed and drained
Few drops of Tabasco or Sriracha
    (optional)
Sea salt and freshly ground
    black pepper

Serves 4

It may seem counterintuitive to use a can of beans to make baked beans, but trust me on this. Proper, homecooked baked beans have about as much in common with the ready-made ones as grocery store sushi has with Tokyo's finest. Instead of a thin, neon-orange sauce, you get a complex dish with the pucker of vinegar, the depth of blackstrap molasses, and the heat of mustard. It's delicious with poached eggs and sausages or crispy bacon, and even with shredded savoy cabbage stirred through.

Heat a large, heavy-bottom saucepan over low-medium heat and add the oil. Add the onion and cook for about 5 minutes until softened, before adding the garlic and cooking for another minute.

Pour in the chopped tomatoes, then add the sugar, blackstrap molasses, mustard, and vinegar, and stir to combine. Simmer for a few minutes over medium heat before adding the beans, and salt and pepper to taste. Reduce the heat to low and partially cover with a lid.

Simmer for 1 hour over low heat, stirring the beans periodically. If the sauce looks like it's becoming too thick and the beans are in danger of sticking to the pot, add a little water to loosen the mixture.

Adjust the seasoning and add a few drops of Tabasco or Sriracha if you like more heat.

CHOCOLATE AND BLUEBERRY OATMEAL WITH TOASTED ALMONDS

½ cup rolled oats

Scant 1 cup almond milk or vanilla rice milk

3 teaspoons unsweetened cocoa

2 teaspoons maple syrup or agave nectar

⅓ cup blueberries, plus extra to sprinkle

Small handful of toasted, slivered almonds, to sprinkle

Serves 1

Oatmeal is one of the best ways to start the day (sorry, bacon). But to keep eating it every weekday morning, I need some fun ingredients. Enter: chocolate. More precisely, unsweetened cocoa–adding chocolate bars wouldn't exactly get the day off to a nourishing, dairy-free start. As the oatmeal heats up, add some blueberries. They'll start to soften and burst, releasing their indigo juices. The whole thing takes less than 10 minutes and makes early mornings bearable.

Place the oats in a small saucepan and add the almond or rice milk. Add the cocoa and maple syrup or agave nectar, stirring until the lumps of cocoa have broken up and are blended in.

Heat for a couple of minutes over low-medium heat, stirring regularly. Add the blueberries after a few minutes; this way they will start to burst but won't lose their shape completely. Bring to a boil briefly, then reduce the heat and simmer for 3 to 4 minutes, stirring well.

Serve with a few extra blueberries and toasted, slivered almonds sprinkled on top.

CACAO NIB AND CRANBERRY GRANOLA

⅓ cup maple syrup
2 teaspoons coconut oil
⅓ cup apple juice
1 teaspoon ground cinnamon
Scant 4½ cups thick rolled oats
⅔ cup pecans, coarsely
   chopped
Scant ½ cup pumpkin seeds
⅓ cup sesame seeds
Pinch of sea salt
⅔ cup dried cranberries
Scant ⅔ cup cacao nibs

Makes 1 ½ pounds

Granola is both easy and fun to make at home (rainy day cooking project alert!). Making it yourself also means you can control what's in it. The dried cranberries in this recipe are both sweet and a little tart at the same time, while cacao nibs add a decadent hint of chocolate but are sugar free and packed full of nutrients. Eat with almond or rice milk, or use in the Bircher Muesli Sundaes (see page 38).

Preheat the oven to 300 °F. Heat the maple syrup, coconut oil, and apple juice in a saucepan over medium heat, stirring occasionally with a wooden spoon, until the oil has melted and the mixture is well-combined.

Grease and line a baking sheet.

Put the cinnamon, oats, pecans, seeds, and salt into a large bowl. Pour in the syrup mixture and stir to coat. Spread this mixture out over the prepared baking sheet, pinching some of it together with your fingers to form small granola clusters.

Bake in the oven for 45 minutes, or until golden brown. Remove from the oven and let cool on the baking sheet. Once it is completely cool, stir in the dried cranberries and cacao nibs. Store in a sterilized Mason jar or an airtight container. It will keep for several weeks. Serve with coconut yogurt, if you like.

BREAKFAST BURRITOS

½ tablespoon olive oil
1 round shallot, finely diced
½ red chile, finely diced
½ teaspoon ground cumin
8 ounces firm tofu, drained and
    patted dry
8 cherry tomatoes, quartered
1 ounce baby leaf spinach
4 medium corn tortillas
1 avocado, halved and finely
    sliced
Small handful of fresh cilantro
    leaves, chopped
Few drops of Tabasco
1 lime, cut into wedges
Sea salt and freshly ground
    black pepper

Serves 2 (makes 4)

Burritos for breakfast—sounds seriously unhealthy, right? Not when we're talking warm corn tortillas filled with scrambled tofu, baby spinach, cherry tomatoes, and creamy avocado. The perkiness of the lime and Tabasco is as good as a caffeine hit.

Heat the oil in a large, heavy-bottom skillet over medium heat. Add the shallot and chile and fry gently for approximately 3 minutes, until the shallot has softened and is turning translucent. Add the cumin and fry for just 30 seconds, until fragrant.

Add the tofu to the pan. Fry for 3 to 4 minutes, until cooked through, using a wooden spoon to break it up until it resembles scrambled eggs. Add the tomatoes and spinach and cook for another 2 minutes, then season generously and remove from the heat.

Meanwhile, place a small skillet over high heat. Add the tortillas one at a time and toast for around 30 seconds on each side until they start to turn golden.

Place a quarter of the tofu, spinach, and tomato mixture onto the middle of each tortilla. Add the avocado slices, sprinkle with a little cilantro, and add a few drops of Tabasco and a squeeze of lime. Fold the sides of the tortilla into the center, on top of the filling. Take the bottom of the tortilla and lift it over the filling, and then roll up. Eat immediately.

CHORIZO AND CHARGRILLED PEPPER MUFFINS

A little olive oil
2 ¼ ounces chorizo, cut into
   small dice
Scant 2 cups self-rising flour
1 teaspoon baking powder
½ teaspoon baking soda
½ teaspoon smoked paprika
Pinch of sea salt
1 egg
½ cup sunflower oil
Scant ½ cup soy or almond milk
⅔ cup plain soy yogurt
4½ ounces chargrilled peppers
   from a jar, cut into ½-inch dice

12-section muffin tray lined with
   12 muffin liners

Makes 12

Chorizo makes everything taste better. Even a small hit of its intensely piggy, spicy flavor lifts stews, soups, and all manner of eggy brunch dishes from average to incredible in the amount of time it takes you to dribble hot, ocher chorizo juice down your chin. My current favorite way of shoehorning chorizo into even more dishes is by adding it to savory baked goods like these easy muffins: a hint of backstreet tapas bar at breakfast time.

Heat a few drops of olive oil in a skillet over medium heat. Add the diced chorizo and fry until crispy. Using a slotted spoon, remove to a plate lined with a few sheets of paper towels to absorb excess oil, and let cool completely.

Preheat the oven to 400 °F. Using a large metal spoon, fold the flour, baking powder, baking soda, smoked paprika, and salt together in a large bowl, until just combined.

Beat the egg, sunflower oil, soy or almond milk, and soy yogurt in a separate bowl, using a fork, until they form a smooth batter. Pour into the dry ingredients and fold in with a large metal spoon, just until the wet ingredients are incorporated; don't overwork the batter. Add the cooled chorizo and diced red pepper and fold in until just combined.

Spoon into the muffin liners and bake in the oven for 15 to 20 minutes, or until the tops are golden. Let cool on a wire rack, in the liners, for 5 to 10 minutes, before serving warm.

ZUCCHINI FRITTERS
WITH POACHED EGGS

1-2 eggs per person
Hot sauce or chili sauce

FOR THE FRITTERS

Generous ¾ cup fine cornmeal
1 teaspoon (gluten-free) baking
  powder
½ teaspoon smoked paprika
2 eggs
2 zucchini (around 14 ounces in
  total), coarsely grated
1 red chile, seeded and finely
  diced
1 scallion (white and green
  part), finely sliced
6 tablespoons vegetable,
  sunflower, or peanut oil
Sea salt and freshly ground
  black pepper

Serves 4 (makes about 10)

These zucchini fritters get extra crunch from being made with cornmeal instead of flour (which makes them gluten free to boot). They make a fine weekend breakfast, drizzled with hot sauce and topped with a poached egg. We've also been known to eat them as "breakfast for dinner," washed down with an ice-cold beer.

Preheat the oven to its lowest setting. Mix together the cornmeal, baking powder, smoked paprika, and eggs with a fork. Pat the grated zucchini dry with paper towels, then stir these into the mixture. Stir in the chile and scallion and season.

Heat the oil in a large, heavy-bottom skillet over medium-high heat. Once hot, spoon in heaping dessert-spoonfuls of the batter and pat down gently into disks, 2 to 3 at a time so the pan doesn't become overcrowded. Fry for 2 to 3 minutes, until golden on the bottom, then flip over with a spatula and cook the other side for 2 to 3 minutes. You may need to add a little more oil to the pan between each batch.

Keep warm in the oven on a plate lined with paper towels until all the fritters are cooked, layering paper towels between each to help soak up oil and keep them crisp.

Meanwhile, poach the eggs. There's the proper way to make poached eggs, and the cheat's way. Here are both:

PROPER WAY: First, use a very fresh egg. Take a tip from food writer Felicity Cloake and break the egg into a small pitcher, and add a drop of white wine vinegar. Bring a saucepan of water to a boil, then whisk the water vigorously to create a whirlpool effect. Stop whisking, then immediately and carefully pour the egg into the center of the whirlpool. Reduce the heat slightly and simmer for 3 minutes.

CHEAT'S WAY: Line a ramekin with a square of plastic wrap about the size of a piece of paper towel. Grease with a little oil using your fingertip, then break an egg into it. Gather up the sides and twist the top to secure. Repeat for as many eggs as you need. Lower these carefully into a pan of simmering water and poach for 4 minutes.

Serve the fritters in small stacks, topped with a poached egg, and perhaps a few drops of chili sauce or your favorite hot sauce.

BLACK FOREST WAFFLES WITH MORELLO CHERRY COMPOTE AND MACADAMIA CREAM

1 ¼ cups all-purpose flour
⅓ cup whole-grain spelt flour
1 ½ teaspoons baking powder
Pinch of sea salt
¼ cup unsweetened cocoa
3 tablespoons superfine sugar
3 eggs
Scant 2 cups almond milk
Generous ⅓ cup dairy-free
   sunflower spread, melted
   and cooled
Vegetable oil, for greasing
Scant ¼ cup semisweet
   chocolate chips

FOR THE MACADAMIA CREAM
1 ⅓ cups blanched macadamias
1 cup cold, filtered water
½ teaspoon vanilla extract
1 ½ teaspoons maple syrup
Pinch of sea salt

FOR THE COMPOTE
14 ounces frozen morello
   cherries or forest fruits
1 tablespoon superfine sugar
Scant 1 cup water

Waffle maker or stovetop
   waffle iron

Serves 4

Frozen Black Forest gateau, with its curls of cheap chocolate and turrets of cream, was a favorite childhood treat of mine. It has long since fallen from fashion, but Black Forest's trinity of chocolate, cherries, and cream is evergreen. These Black Forest waffles are definitely a special-occasion breakfast. The gooey cocoa batter is flecked with nibs of melting dark chocolate and served with a juicy cherry compote and a big dollop of chilled macadamia cream.

For the macadamia cream, the night before, place the macadamias in a large bowl. Add enough cold water from the faucet to cover the nuts, cover the bowl, and let soak overnight.

The next morning, rinse and drain the nuts and put them in a blender with the 1 cup filtered water. Add the vanilla, maple syrup, and salt and blitz until you have a thick cream, then refrigerate until needed.

For the waffles, sift both flours, the baking powder, salt, cocoa powder, and sugar into a large bowl. Beat the eggs, almond milk, and cooled, melted cream together. Whisk into the flour mixture and continue whisking until you have a smooth, lump-free batter. Let stand for 10 minutes. Preheat the oven to its lowest setting.

Make the compote by putting the frozen fruits, sugar, and water into a saucepan. Bring to a boil briefly, then turn the heat down slightly and simmer until the fruits have softened and you have a thick compote. Remove from the heat and cover to keep warm.

Preheat the waffle maker or the stovetop waffle iron and lightly grease with vegetable oil. Stir the chocolate chips into the rested batter, then ladle in the correct amount of batter for your hot waffle maker, making sure you ladle out a few chocolate chips for each waffle if they have sunk to the bottom. Cook until crisp on the outside, and keep warm on a plate lined with paper towels in the oven on the lowest setting while you make the rest of the waffles.

Serve in stacks with a big dollop of the macadamia cream and the compote on the side.

CHAI FRENCH TOAST WITH CINNAMON-ROASTED PEARS

1 cup almond or vanilla
  rice milk
4 eggs
1 ½ tablespoons superfine sugar
1 teaspoon ground ginger
½ teaspoon ground cinnamon
2 cardamom pods, lightly
  crushed
1 teaspoon ground nutmeg
2 cloves
Pinch of sea salt and a generous
  twist of black pepper
4 thick slices of slightly stale,
  good white bread
2 tablespoons sunflower or
  canola oil
Granulated sugar, to sprinkle
Coconut yogurt, to serve

FOR THE PEARS
1 tablespoon light olive oil, plus
  extra for greasing
2 teaspoons soft brown sugar
1 teaspoon ground cinnamon
1 teaspoon vanilla extract
4 small pears, peeled, halved
  lengthwise, and seeds removed

Serves 4

Golden-crusted French toast, scented with chai spices. Pair it (forgive the pun) with juicy roasted pears and you have a recipe for pure breakfast indulgence.

Whisk together the almond or rice milk, eggs, sugar, spices, salt, and pepper in a mixing pitcher and let infuse while you make the pear mixture.

Preheat the oven to 350 °F. Line a baking sheet with foil and drizzle with a few drops of olive oil.

For the pear mixture, combine the oil, sugar, cinnamon, and vanilla in a bowl. Toss the pear halves in this mixture to coat. Place on the foil-lined sheet, drizzle with any remaining cinnamon mixture, and roast in the preheated oven for 25 minutes or until golden and tender in the middle, turning them over halfway through cooking. Remove from the oven and cover with foil to keep warm while you make the custard mixture.

Pour the milk-and-egg mixture into a medium-size baking dish and pick out the whole spices. Whisk again to make sure the spices don't cling to the side of the dish. Lay the slices of bread in the liquid and soak for 30 seconds, pressing down lightly with a wooden spoon. Turn over and soak the other side for 30 to 60 seconds (you may need to do this in batches, depending on the size of your dish). Transfer to a plate.

Heat the oil in a large, heavy-bottom skillet over medium-high heat. Add a slice of the soaked bread and fry for about 3 minutes, until golden on the bottom. Don't move it during this time, so it can form a good crust. Sprinkle the top with a little granulated sugar, then flip over and cook the other side until golden. Transfer to a plate and cover with foil to keep warm while you repeat with the remaining slices of soaked bread.

Serve with two pear halves on top of each slice of toast and a dollop of coconut yogurt.

APRICOT AND PISTACHIO
BREAKFAST BREAD

½ cup shelled pistachio kernels

Generous 1 cup self-rising flour, sifted

½ cup + 2 tablespoons cornmeal

1 teaspoon baking powder

Pinch of salt

¾ cup dried apricots, finely diced into approximately ⅛-inch cubes

1 cup olive oil

1 cup superfine sugar

4 eggs

2-pound loaf pan

Makes 1 large loaf

Bake this simple loaf cake ahead of time when you're expecting a crowd for brunch. Leftovers can be sliced and frozen, then toasted under the broiler and spread with a little coconut oil or coconut butter. The cornmeal adds texture and a little crunch, and the loaf is flecked with sweet apricots and delicious toasted pistachios.

Toast the pistachio kernels in a dry skillet over medium heat, until they start to turn golden (keep a careful eye on them as they can easily burn). Remove to a plate and let cool. Once completely cool, coarsely chop into small pieces.

Grease and line the loaf pan with wax paper.

Preheat the oven to 350 °F.

Sift the flour, cornmeal, baking powder, and salt together in a large bowl. Scoop out 2 tablespoons of this mixture and use to coat the apricot and pistachio pieces; this is important to stop the fruit and nuts from sinking in the cake batter. Set aside.

Beat the olive oil and sugar together with an electric whisk in another large bowl or with the paddle attachment of a stand mixer for a couple of minutes, until well combined.

Add the eggs one at a time, alternating with a tablespoon of the flour mixture, and keep whisking to combine.

Fold in the rest of the flour mixture using a large metal spoon, until just combined. Fold in the flour-covered apricots and pistachios.

Pour the mixture into the loaf pan and smooth the top. Bake for 50 to 60 minutes, or until the top is golden and a skewer or toothpick inserted into the middle comes out clean. Let cool in the pan for 5 minutes before turning out onto a wire rack to cool completely.

Serve with a dollop of coconut yogurt. Slice any leftover breakfast bread and freeze.

BIRCHER MUESLI SUNDAES

1¾ cups whole rolled oats
2 tablespoons slivered almonds,
    chopped
2 tablespoons lemon juice
Scant 1 cup water
⅔ cup coconut yogurt
1 teaspoon maple syrup or honey
    (optional)
Granola (see cacao nib and
    cranberry granola on page 28)
Fresh blueberries
Fresh strawberries, sliced

1 tall sundae glass per person

*Serves 4 to 6, depending on the
    size of your glasses*

There aren't many dishes served in sundae glasses that can be
legitimately called healthy, but here's one. I got the idea for these
from a sweet, 1950s-style café in Melbourne, where they serve Bircher
and blackberries in tall glasses, to be eaten with a long sundae spoon
and washed down with a strong coffee.

The night before, mix the oats and slivered almonds together with
the lemon juice and water in a large bowl. Cover and leave in the
refrigerator.

The next morning, stir the coconut yogurt into the mixture to make
the Bircher. Sweeten with the maple syrup or honey, if you like, but
remember that the granola and berries will both bring sweetness to
the dish.

Make sundaes by layering alternate layers of Bircher muesli, granola,
and berries in each sundae glass. Top with a final layer of berries and
a scattering of slivered almonds, and eat with long sundae spoons.

DAIRY-FREE MILKS

Make your own milks, if you can, as most bought versions contain oils and stabilizers. If using almond milk in cooking, keep it plain with a pinch of salt; if not, then it is much yummier with a little maple or agave syrup or honey, and spices like cinnamon and nutmeg. Cashew milk is—in my opinion—the most delicious. When boosted by vanilla, maple, and sea salt, it has a pleasant, cookie taste. The oat milk will turn out creamier and thicker than a store-bought one and it benefits from a little maple syrup and vanilla. Rice milk is a little thin to use in cooking but it works well on cereal and in drinks. Please note, that in the UK rice milk is not recommended for children under 5 years. For all the milks except the rice one, you can use the meal left behind in the sieve to stir into Bircher muesli, oatmeal, smoothies, or coconut yogurt.

ALMOND MILK

1 1/3 cups whole, unsalted
  almonds, skin on
2 1/2 cups cold, filtered water
Pinch of sea salt

FOR SWEETENED MILK
1 tablespoon maple syrup
1/2 teaspoon ground cinnamon
  and/or nutmeg
1 1/2 teaspoons vanilla extract

Makes about 2 cups (use the ratio of 1:3 nuts to water to make more or less milk)

Place the almonds in a large bowl. Add enough cold water to cover the nuts, cover the bowl, and let soak for 8 hours or overnight.

Drain the almonds and rinse well. Place in a blender and add the cold, filtered water and the salt. Add the maple syrup, cinnamon or nutmeg, and vanilla, if making sweetened milk. Blitz until the almonds are broken up into very small pieces and you have a creamy liquid. Place a strainer over a large bowl and line with a piece of cheesecloth. Pour the almond milk mixture into the cheesecloth-lined strainer and press down firmly with a spoon to push all the liquid through into the bowl, leaving the nut meal in the strainer. If the milk still has bits of nuts in it, pour it back through the strainer. Store in an airtight container in the refrigerator for 2 days. Shake well before using.

RICE MILK

1 cup brown or white rice
2 1/2 cups cold, filtered water
Pinch of sea salt

FOR SWEETENED MILK
1 tablespoon maple syrup
1 1/2 tablespoons vanilla extract

Makes about 2 1/3 cups (use the ratio of 1:3 rice to water to make more or less milk)

Place the rice in a large bowl and cover with double the volume of cold water. Let soak for 8 hours or overnight.

The next day, drain and thoroughly rinse the rice. Place the rice in a blender and add the filtered water and the salt. Add the maple syrup and vanilla, if making sweetened milk. Blitz until the rice is broken up into very small pieces and you have a creamy liquid. Place a fine-mesh strainer over a large mixing bowl and line with a piece of cheesecloth. Pour the liquid and rice meal into the cheesecloth-lined strainer. Press down firmly with a spoon to push the last of the liquid into the bowl, leaving the rice meal behind. Discard the rice.

OAT MILK

2 ⅓ cups rolled oats (look for gluten-free oats if you want to ensure this is gluten free, too)
2 ½ cups cold, filtered water
Pinch of sea salt

FOR SWEETENED MILK
1 tablespoon maple syrup
½ teaspoon ground cinnamon and/or nutmeg
1 ½ teaspoons vanilla extract

Makes about 2 cups (use the ratio of 1:3 oats to water to make more or less milk)

Soak the oats in the filtered water for 1 hour. Strain the liquid into a blender, then rinse the softened oats before adding them to the blender with the salt. Add the maple syrup, spices, and vanilla, if making sweetened milk. Blitz until smooth.

Place a fine-mesh strainer over a large mixing bowl. Pour the oat mixture into the strainer and press down with a wooden spoon to push all the liquid through the oats into the bowl. Transfer the oat mixture to a separate bowl and use to make oatmeal. If the oat milk still has pieces of oats in it, you can pour it back through the strainer. Use on oatmeal and cereal, and in smoothies and drinks. It keeps for up to a week in an airtight container in the refrigerator. Shake well before using.

CASHEW MILK

1 ⅓ cups unsalted cashews
2 ½ cups cold, filtered water
Pinch of sea salt
1 tablespoon maple syrup
1 ½ teaspoons vanilla extract

Makes around 2 cups (use the ratio of 1:3 nuts to water to make more or less milk)

Put the cashews in a large bowl. Add enough cold water to cover the nuts, cover the bowl, and let soak for 8 hours or overnight.

Drain the cashews, rinse well, and place in a blender. Add the cold, filtered water, salt, maple syrup, and vanilla (or for unsweetened milk, omit these last two). Blitz until the cashews are broken up into very small pieces and you have a pale, creamy liquid. Place a fine-mesh strainer over a large bowl and line with a piece of cheesecloth. Pour the cashew milk mixture into the cheesecloth-lined strainer and press down firmly with a spoon to push all the liquid through into the bowl, leaving the nut meal in the strainer. If the milk still has bits of nuts in it, pour it back through the strainer. Store in an airtight container in the refrigerator for a couple of days. Shake well before using.

ALTERNATIVES: To make chocolate milk, add 2 teaspoons unsweetened cocoa to the blender with the nuts, water, salt, maple syrup, and vanilla (omit the spices). To make gingerbread milk, add 1½ teaspoons ground ginger and ½ teaspoon ground nutmeg to the blender with the nuts, water, salt, maple syrup, and vanilla.

LUNCH

ULTIMATE FISH FINGER SANDWICH WITH CHIPOTLE MAYO AND ARUGULA

FOR THE FISH FINGERS

7 ounces sustainable white fish
    fillets, such as cod
¼ cup all-purpose flour
1 egg, beaten
½ cup panko bread crumbs
3 tablespoons vegetable or
    sunflower oil
Sea salt and freshly ground
    black pepper

FOR THE SANDWICHES

1 teaspoon chipotle paste
2 tablespoons good-quality
    mayonnaise (check the label
    to make sure it's dairy free)
4 slices white sourdough bread
1 handful of fresh arugula

Serves 2

The fish finger sandwich is a British classic. Food historians trace its roots back to the 1980s, the golden era of frozen dinners and suspiciously orange bread crumbs. It was a time when we weren't afraid to double-carb by stuffing fish fingers inside bendy white bread. As much as store-bought fish fingers are still a guilty pleasure, homemade ones, coated in crisp panko and sandwiched between fresh sourdough, are in another league altogether.

Preheat the oven to its lowest setting.

Skin the fish fillets if necessary and cut into strips ¾–1¼ inches wide, using a sharp knife.

Mix the flour with some salt and pepper on a plate. Put the bowl of beaten egg next to it, the panko bread crumbs on another plate next to that, and finally a clean plate. Using kitchen tongs, roll the fish strips in the seasoned flour to coat. Shake off any excess and then carefully dip in the beaten egg with the tongs, before rolling in the panko bread crumbs—each "finger" should be thoroughly coated with the bread crumbs. Place the fish fingers on the clean plate.

Heat the oil in a large, heavy-bottom skillet over high heat. Test whether the oil is hot enough by dropping in a bread crumb—it should start sizzling immediately. Add the fish fingers to the hot oil and fry in a couple of batches for 2 to 3 minutes on each side until the bread crumbs are crisp and golden and the fish is cooked through. Use the kitchen tongs to lift the fish fingers and brown the sides. Keep the first batch warm on a plate in the oven on the lowest setting.

Meanwhile, mix the chipotle paste and mayonnaise together in a bowl. Cut the sourdough slices in half and spread the chipotle mayo on each. Add a small handful of arugula to one half and top with a couple of fish fingers and the other half slice of bread. Serve immediately.

CAESAR SALAD

2 tablespoons olive oil
1-2 slices sourdough or good-
   quality white bread, cut into
   ¾-inch cubes
1 large Romaine lettuce,
   divided into leaves
1 tablespoon toasted, slivered
   almonds
Sea salt and freshly ground
   black pepper

FOR THE DRESSING
1 ½ teaspoons Worcestershire
   sauce
2 anchovy fillets in oil, chopped
1 garlic clove
Finely grated zest of 1 lemon
   and the juice of ½
4 tablespoons good-quality
   mayonnaise (check the label
   to make sure it's dairy free)

Serves 4

There was a time in the 1990s and aughts when you couldn't avoid Caesar salad. It may not have the fashion clout of kale and quinoa, but a good Caesar is still just as delicious as it was back then. Here, toasted, slivered almonds take the place of Parmesan, and the creamy dressing makes eating a big plate of lettuce a pleasure. For a more substantial salad, add pieces of broiled chicken and/or crispy bacon.

Heat the oil in a small, heavy-bottom skillet over medium-high heat. Add the bread cubes, sprinkle with salt, and fry until golden, using kitchen tongs to turn them over to ensure all sides are cooked. Transfer to a plate lined with paper towels and set aside.

To make the dressing, blitz the Worcestershire sauce, chopped anchovies, garlic, and lemon zest in a small food processor (you want a paste, but some texture is fine). Spoon into a bowl and add the lemon juice and mayonnaise. Whisk until you have a smooth dressing, then season to taste.

Toss the dressing with the lettuce and slivered almonds in a bowl until well coated. Divide between four plates, top with the croutons, and serve.

COUSCOUS WITH TOASTED ALMONDS AND CRISPY KALE

2 tablespoons olive oil
Scant 1½ cups couscous
Finely grated zest of 1 lemon
1¾ cups hot chicken or
    vegetable broth
3½ ounces curly kale, any woody
    stalks removed
½ cup toasted, slivered almonds
Sea salt

FOR THE DRESSING
3 tablespoons extra-virgin
    olive oil
1 tablespoon lemon juice
½ tablespoon soy sauce

Serves 4

This easy side dish packs a lot of flavor thanks to the salty, crispy kale, lemon zest, and the secret ingredient in the dressing: soy sauce. Make it a filling meal by serving with chicken drumsticks or sausages. Any leftovers will keep in the refrigerator for lunchboxes the following day.

Heat 1 tablespoon of the oil in a large, heavy-bottom pan (that has a lid) over medium-high heat. Add the couscous and fry gently for 2 minutes, stirring to coat all the grains.

Add the lemon zest, then pour in the broth. Stir once, then remove from the heat, cover, and leave for 5 to 10 minutes.

Meanwhile, heat the remaining tablespoon of oil in a heavy-bottom skillet. Add the curly kale, sprinkle with salt, and stir-fry until dark and crispy, for about 5 minutes.

Whisk together the dressing ingredients. Pour over the couscous and stir, before adding the crispy kale and almonds. Serve immediately.

PULLED PORK BELLY CEMITAS

**FOR THE PULLED
PORK BELLY**
1 ¾ pounds pork belly joint
1 tablespoon olive oil
1 tablespoon sea salt
1 tablespoon soft brown sugar
1 teaspoon chipotle paste

FOR THE CEMITAS
2 avocados
4 teaspoons lime juice
1 garlic clove, crushed
4 seeded burger buns (check the
   ingredients to make sure they
   are dairy free)
A few sprigs of fresh papalo
   (Mexican herb) or cilantro
   leaves
Sea salt

Makes 4

The *cemita* is a sandwich from Mexico's Puebla region. In its classic form, avocado, meat (beef or pork), panela cheese, and perhaps a little salsa roja are crammed into a seeded egg roll. With a little tinkering I've made a dairy-free version with extra flavor courtesy of pulled pork belly, shards of crackling, and a little chipotle.

Preheat the oven to 400 °F.

Pat the pork belly dry with paper towels and score the skin using a sharp paring knife. Rub the oil into the skin and then rub half of the salt and sugar in. Turn the pork belly over and rub the rest of the salt and sugar into the other side of the meat.

Place the pork belly skin side up in a roasting pan and roast for 30 minutes, then reduce the oven temperature to 300 °F and cook for another 3 ½ hours. Remove from the oven and pull the meat away from the skin. It should be soft and come away easily in shreds; set aside.

Increase the oven temperature back up to 400 °F and return the pork skin to the oven in the roasting pan. Roast until you have crispy crackling, for about 15 to 20 minutes. Remove from the oven and let cool slightly, then use a sharp knife to cut it into small pieces. Stir the chipotle paste into the shredded pork.

Mash the avocados with the lime juice and garlic, and season with a little salt. Slice and lightly broil or toast the buns.

To assemble, spread a generous amount of mashed avocado on the bottom half of each bun and just a little on the top. Arrange the pulled pork on top and sprinkle with a few pieces of crackling. Top with papalo or cilantro, then with the other half of the bun.

CRISPY KALE, BUTTERNUT SQUASH, AND PECAN RED QUINOA SALAD

1 cup red quinoa
2 tablespoons olive oil
11 ounces butternut squash, chopped into ¾-inch cubes
4 ounces curly kale, woody stalks removed
½ cup pecans
1 heaping teaspoon rosemary needles
Scant ½ cup dried cranberries
Sea salt

TO DRESS
2 teaspoons extra-virgin olive oil
Juice of ½ lemon

Serves 4

When I lived in NYC, our "kitchen" was a toaster oven and a hot plate. This nourishing, simple supper was something that could be made in a couple of pans, using the colorful squashes, cranberries, and nuts piled high in the local grocery store, and will always remind me of a New York fall. (See photograph on page 42.)

Place the quinoa in a saucepan and cover with twice its volume of cold water. Bring to a boil, turn the heat down, cover, and simmer for 18 to 20 minutes, until all the water is absorbed. Once cooked, fluff up the grains using a fork.

Meanwhile, heat the oil in a large, heavy-bottom skillet and add the cubed butternut. Cook over high heat for 10 minutes, then add the kale, sprinkle with salt, and fry for another 10 minutes, or until the kale is crispy and the squash is cooked through.

Toast the pecans with the rosemary and a little salt in a hot, dry skillet, until they turn golden and release wonderful, toasty aromas; keep a careful eye on them to prevent burning. Remove from the heat, coarsely chop, and tip onto a plate to cool.

Assemble the salad on each plate by dividing the quinoa between them and adding the kale, squash, and pecans. Sprinkle with dried cranberries, dress with the oil and lemon juice, and serve.

THAI-STYLE FISHCAKES
WITH CRUSHED PEAS

9 ounces boneless salmon fillets,
  skinned and diced
11–12 ounces skinless, boneless,
  sustainable white fish fillets
  such as cod, diced
1 garlic clove
1 teaspoon soft brown sugar
1 egg
1 teaspoon chopped fresh ginger
1 teaspoon fish sauce
1 teaspoon soy sauce
1 red chile, seeded and finely
  diced
1 scallion (white and green
  part), finely chopped
2 kaffir lime leaves, minced
Small handful of fresh cilantro,
  chopped
Peanut, vegetable, or
  sunflower oil, for frying
Sea salt and freshly ground
  black pepper

FOR THE PEAS
4 1/3 cups frozen peas
4 tablespoons peanut or
  light olive oil
1/2 red chile, seeded and minced
Juice of 1/2 lime
Small handful of fresh cilantro
  (leaves and stalks), minced

*Serves 4 as a main course or
8 as an appetizer*

Thai fishcakes (or *tod man pla*) have become a classic appetizer in recent decades. This recipe makes larger fishcakes for an easy main course, served on a bed of peas lightly crushed with fresh chile and lime. If you want to serve them as an appetizer, just divide the mixture into 6 or 8 smaller patties. They're a boon for gluten-free guests, too, as they're one of the few fishcakes not coated in bread crumbs ...

Put all the fish with the garlic, sugar, egg, ginger, fish sauce, and soy sauce in a food processor and mix to a coarse paste (it should still have some texture). Transfer to a large bowl and mix in the chile, scallion, lime leaves, and cilantro. Season generously with salt and black pepper, divide the mixture into 4, and bring together with your hands to form thick, flat, round patties.

Pour enough oil to form a 3/4-inch layer in a large, heavy-bottom skillet. Heat over high heat until it starts to shimmer. Slide in the fishcakes with a spatula and fry for 4 to 5 minutes on each side until golden on the outside and cooked through. You may need to do this in batches, depending on the size of your pan.

Meanwhile, cook the peas in a saucepan of simmering water, until tender. Drain and transfer to a bowl with the oil, chile, and lime juice. Mash lightly with a potato masher so they still retain some texture. Stir in the cilantro and season.

Serve each fishcake on top of a spoonful of crushed peas.

BANH XEO

1 ¼ cups rice flour, sifted
2 teaspoons ground turmeric
Scant 1 cup coconut milk
Generous pinch of sea salt
1 cup water
Vegetable, peanut, or
    canola oil, for frying
½ onion, thinly sliced
2 ¾ ounces shiitake mushrooms,
    thinly sliced
6 ½ ounces raw king shrimp
1 ½ cups bean sprouts
1 scallion (white and green
    part), finely sliced on the
    diagonal

**FOR THE DIPPING SAUCE
(NUOC MAM PHA)**
2 tablespoons lime juice
Scant ¼ cup fish sauce
Scant 1 cup lukewarm water
¼ cup superfine sugar
1 large red chile, minced
2 garlic cloves, minced

TO SERVE
Lettuce leaves
A handful of fresh cilantro,
    mint, and Thai basil leaves

Serves 4

Banh xeo is a crisp and lacy pancake from Vietnam. This savory crêpe is traditionally filled with pork and shrimp (though for an easy lunch I've left out the pork), vegetables, and bean sprouts. Depending on where you are in Vietnam, it is made with or without coconut milk. I was taught to make it with just water but prefer the subtle coconut flavor that comes from using a mixture of the two …

Whisk together the rice flour, turmeric, coconut milk, and salt. Slowly add the water until you have a thin, lump-free batter, about the consistency of light cream. Let stand for 20 minutes.

Meanwhile, to make the dipping sauce, whisk together the lime juice, fish sauce, and water. Add the sugar and whisk until it dissolves, then add the chile and garlic and stir to combine. Check that all the sugar has dissolved, then let it stand.

Heat a nonstick skillet or sauté pan (that has a lid) over medium-high heat. Heat 1 tablespoon oil, then fry the onion and mushrooms until the onions are softened and the mushrooms are turning golden, then remove to a plate. Add the shrimp to the pan and fry until pink and cooked through. Remove to the plate.

Pour a little oil into the pan, swirl the pan around, then pat with paper towels to give the bottom an even covering. Turn the heat up to high; then, when the oil is very hot, pour in enough pancake batter to make a thin coating on the bottom of the pan. Swirl the pan around so the batter evenly coats the bottom, then add a small handful of the cooked onion, mushrooms, and shrimp, with some bean sprouts and scallion. Cover with a lid and cook until the pancake turns very crisp. It should be golden at the edges and coming away from the pan.

Remove the lid and use a spatula to fold one half of the pancake over the other. Carefully slide onto a plate and serve immediately with plenty of lettuce leaves, cilantro, mint, and Thai basil (if you can get hold of it), with the dipping sauce in small bowls on the side. The traditional way to eat *banh xeo* is to take a lettuce leaf, pile some herbs onto it, then break off a piece of the pancake and place it inside the leaf. Roll it up like an egg roll and dip into the sauce.

AVOCADO AND RADISH QUINOA TABBOULEH

Generous ¾ cup quinoa
⅔ cup cold water
1 avocado, peeled and cut into
   ½-inch cubes
8 radishes, finely sliced
1 stalk of celery, finely sliced
1 scallion (white and green
   part), sliced on the diagonal
1 large bunch (about 1 ounce) of
   flat-leaf parsley (including
   stalks), minced
1 teaspoon mint leaves, minced
Finely grated zest and juice
   of ½ lemon
1½ tablespoons extra-virgin
   olive oil
Sea salt and freshly ground
   black pepper

*Serves 2 as a light lunch
or 4 as a side dish*

This salad, what with the quinoa and the avocado, won't win any authenticity points in Beirut, but creamy avocado and peppery radish make excellent additions to an herby tabbouleh.

Place the quinoa in a saucepan and cover with the water. Bring to a boil, then turn the heat down to medium, cover, and simmer for 10 to 15 minutes, until the grains are plumped up and have absorbed all the water yet still retain a little crunch. Set aside to cool.

Tip the cooled quinoa into a large serving bowl. Add the avocado, radishes, celery, scallion, parsley, mint, and lemon zest. Season with salt and pepper and mix well to combine. Add the olive oil and lemon juice and stir into the salad.

CREAMY CHICKEN SOUP

1 ½ tablespoons olive oil
½ onion, finely diced
1 large leek, trimmed and finely
   sliced
2 carrots, finely diced
7 ounces leftover roasted
   chicken, skinned and cut
   into small chunks
2 ½ cups hot chicken broth
⅔ cup oat cream
½ tablespoon mustard powder
Squeeze of lemon juice
Large handful of flat-leaf parsley,
   chopped
Sea salt and freshly ground
   black pepper

Serves 4

A filling and creamy chicken soup for rainy days, cold nights, and any time you need a bit of comfort in a bowl. Use ready-cooked chicken if you don't have any left over from the weekend roast ...

Heat the oil in a heavy-bottom saucepan over medium heat. Fry the onion gently for 3 to 4 minutes. Add the leek and carrots and fry for another 10 minutes, until the vegetables are softened.

Add the chicken and pour in the broth. Bring to a boil, then reduce the heat, cover, and simmer for 20 minutes.

Remove 2 large spoonfuls of the chicken and vegetables and set aside on a plate. Blitz the soup with a stick blender or in a food processor until smooth. Return to the pan, if necessary, and add the reserved chicken and vegetables, then stir in the oat cream and mustard powder.

Season generously and add the lemon juice. Stir in most of the parsley, sprinkle the rest on top, and serve immediately.

PARSNIP, CARROT, AND SWEET POTATO SOUP WITH SOURDOUGH CROUTONS

FOR THE SOUP

1 1/2 tablespoons vegetable or
    canola oil
1 onion, diced
1 red chile, seeded and finely
    diced
1 1/2 teaspoons smoked paprika
1 teaspoon dried oregano
1 3/4 pounds root vegetables, a
    mixture of parsnips, carrots,
    and sweet potatoes, peeled
    and diced
5 cups hot chicken or vegetable
    broth
1 cup red lentils
Extra-virgin olive oil, to serve
Sea salt and freshly ground
    black pepper

FOR THE CROUTONS

3 slices day-old white sourdough
    bread
3 tablespoons vegetable or
    canola oil

Serves 4

There's so much goodness in this soup. The root vegetables and red lentils are packed with vitamins and fiber, and the mixture of yellow and amber ingredients is like a bowl of sunshine on a cold, gray day. Just in case it was all seeming too worthy, you've got musky heat from the chile and smoked paprika, a little naughtiness in the form of the golden, crunchy croutons, and a swirl of rich olive oil to finish things off.

Heat the oil in a large, heavy-bottom saucepan over medium heat. Sauté the onion for 5 minutes until softened and translucent. Add the chile and cook for 1 minute, then add the smoked paprika and oregano and cook, stirring, for 30 seconds or so, until the paprika starts to release its fragrance.

Stir in the diced root vegetables and cook for another 2 minutes. Pour in the broth and add the lentils. Bring to a boil, then turn the heat down and simmer, covered, for about 20 minutes until all the vegetables are softened.

Season with plenty of salt and some black pepper, remove from the heat and blend to a smooth soup in a blender (you will probably need to do this in batches) or with a stick blender.

Meanwhile, heat the oil for the croutons in a skillet over high heat. Test whether the oil is ready by adding one bread cube. If it starts sizzling and spitting immediately, then add the other cubes. Fry for 2 to 3 minutes, turning regularly with a wooden spoon or spatula, until golden. Transfer to a plate lined with paper towels and sprinkle with salt.

Divide the soup between four bowls. Garnish each with a swirl of extra-virgin olive oil and a handful of croutons.

SEAFOOD CHOWDER

1 tablespoon light olive oil
1 onion, finely diced
2 ½ cups hot fish broth
10 ½ ounces waxy potatoes,
    peeled and cut into
    ½-inch cubes
1 ¾ cups coconut milk
¾ teaspoon smoked paprika
10 ounces smoked white fish,
    such as cod
5¾ ounces responsibly sourced
    scallops
5½ ounces raw king shrimp
1 ¾ cups frozen corn, thawed
    and drained
Squeeze of lime
Handful of fresh cilantro,
    coarsely chopped, to serve
Sea salt and freshly ground
    black pepper

Serves 4 to 6

A velvety chowder packed with scallops and shrimp, and with a hint of Mexico courtesy of the smoky heat from the paprika, the corn, and freshly squeezed lime ...

Heat the oil in a large, heavy-bottom saucepan, and fry the onion gently for a few minutes until softened.

Pour in the broth, then add the potatoes. Bring to a boil briefly, then turn the heat down and simmer until the potatoes are tender.

Stir in the coconut milk, then the smoked paprika. Flake in the smoked fish, add the scallops and shrimp, and simmer for about 4 minutes until they are all cooked through. Add the corn and simmer for another minute.

Season, add a squeeze of lime, and serve topped with cilantro.

LEMON SOLE PACKAGES
WITH RICE NOODLE SALAD

2 tablespoons soy sauce
1 tablespoon lime juice
1 tablespoon honey
1 tablespoon peanut or
    canola oil, plus extra
    for drizzling
4 lemon sole fillets
Lime wedges, to serve

FOR THE SALAD
3 ½ ounces rice vermicelli
    noodles
Peanut or sesame oil,
    for drizzling
2 medium carrots, cut into
    ¾-inch matchsticks
1 scallion (white and green
    part), thinly sliced on the
    diagonal
½ red chile, seeded and
    finely diced
Large handful of cilantro
    (leaves and stalks), coarsely
    chopped
2 tablespoons lime juice
1 tablespoon fish sauce
1 tablespoon soy sauce
2 teaspoons superfine sugar
Large handful of salted peanuts,
    coarsley chopped

Serves 4

Delicate lemon sole fillets glazed with lime, soy, and honey, partnered with a Thai-style rice noodle salad. This light and easy lunch is on the table in 20 minutes.

Preheat the oven to 400 °F.

Mix the soy sauce, lime juice, honey, and oil together to form a glaze. Brush a light coating of the glaze onto the top side of each sole fillet. Cut out 4 squares of foil large enough to form a package around each fish fillet. Drizzle a few drops of oil in each and lay a fillet on top. Drizzle any extra glaze on top. Fold the sides of the foil over the fish and scrunch together at the top to form a package. Place on a baking sheet and bake for 10 minutes until the fish is cooked through.

Meanwhile, place the noodles in a large bowl. Pour over boiling water and let soak for 10 minutes, or until tender but still with some bite. Drain, rinse in cold water, and drain again. Toss the noodles with a little oil. Add the carrots, scallion, chile, and most of the cilantro.

Whisk together the lime juice, fish sauce, soy sauce, and sugar in a bowl. Toss this dressing into the noodles, then sprinkle with the peanuts and the remaining cilantro.

To serve, squeeze a little extra lime juice from one lime wedge onto each fish fillet and serve the remaining lime wedges on the side.

SLOW-ROASTED TOMATO AND HARISSA TART

1 pound, 2 ounces ripe but firm
vine tomatoes,
a mixture of red and yellow,
cut into ½-inch slices
1 teaspoon ground cumin
1 teaspoon ground coriander
1 tablespoon olive oil
Pinch of sea salt
11 ½-ounces sheet of ready-made
puff pastry (NOT the
all-butter kind)
4 tablespoons tomato purée
2 teaspoons harissa paste
Baby spinach leaves, to garnish

Serves 4 to 6

Ready-made puff pastry is a nifty standby ingredient, allowing you to make impressive tarts and pastries in a hurry. Most food writers will implore readers to use an all-butter pastry, but sadly that's no use for those of us avoiding dairy. Luckily, most stores also sell puff pastry made with vegetable oil and, I'll be honest, I can barely taste the difference between the two. This simple tomato tart has a North African influence thanks to the harissa paste and the earthy coriander and cumin, which contrast nicely with the sweet jamminess of the roasted tomatoes.

Preheat the oven to 275 °F.

Mix together the sliced tomatoes, cumin, and coriander in a large bowl with the oil and salt, until all the slices are nicely coated with oil and spices.

Spread out the tomato slices on a baking sheet. Roast for 30 minutes until the edges are slightly crisp but the middles are still soft and juicy. Remove from the oven and set aside. Increase the oven temperature to 400 °F.

Roll out the sheet of pastry onto a baking sheet and score a border 1 ¼ inches in from the edge. Mix the passata and harissa paste together in a bowl, then spread this mixture on the pastry inside the border. Place the tomatoes on top haphazardly (or in neat vertical rows if you prefer), overlapping each other and staying inside the border.

Bake for 20 minutes or until cooked through and the crust is puffy and golden. Garnish with baby spinach leaves and serve with new potatoes and a crisp green salad.

ROASTED CHICKEN, TOASTED HAZELNUT, AND APPLE ON SOURDOUGH

⅓ cup blanched hazelnuts
3 tablespoons good-quality
  mayonnaise (check the label
  to make sure it's dairy free)
1½ teaspoons lemon juice
5½ ounces leftover roasted
  chicken, chopped into
  small chunks
Small handful of flat-leaf parsley
  leaves, chopped
½ crisp red apple, cut into
  small chunks
Handful of Boston lettuce
  leaves
4 slices good sourdough bread,
  sliced
Sea salt and freshly ground
  black pepper

Makes 2 large sandwiches

To make this sandwich, you're going to need some leftover roasted chicken (most likely from Sunday lunch, making it the perfect Monday-blues-fighting sandwich). There are lots of delicious flavors here—the toasted hazelnuts, the tender chicken, and sharpness from the red apple and lemon. If you're debating whether it's worth roasting a chicken just to make this sandwich … yes. Yes it is.

Toast the hazelnuts in a small, dry skillet over medium-high heat until they turn golden and start to crack—keep a careful eye on them as they can burn quickly. Tip onto a plate and let cool before coarsely chopping.

Mix the mayonnaise and lemon juice together in a large bowl and season to taste. Stir in the chicken, parsley, cooled hazelnuts, and diced apple.

Place a lettuce leaf, or more if small, on a slice of bread, top with the chicken salad, and another slice of bread. Alternatively, these are delicious (albeit messy) as toasted open sandwiches.

POTATO SALAD WITH CHORIZO CRUMBS

2 ¼ pounds new potatoes, rinsed and halved

1 teaspoon olive oil

2¾ ounces chorizo, cut into small cubes the size of large bread crumbs

Scant ¼ cup panko bread crumbs

4 tablespoons good-quality mayonnaise (check the label to make sure it's dairy free)

2 teaspoons lemon juice

2 scallions (white and green parts), minced

Sea salt and freshly ground black pepper

Serves 6

This potato salad is inspired by the migas dishes you find all over Spain—fried bread crumbs that were once "cooked on little braziers" by shepherds, according to cookbook writer Claudia Roden. These days they're a tapas bar staple, fried in olive oil (or sometimes pork fat). Here I've combined small crumbs of chorizo with crispy panko, which hungrily soak up the fiery rust-colored oil from the sausage. They taste absolutely delicious sprinkled over potato salad.

Add the potatoes to a large pan of boiling, salted water. Return to a boil, then turn the heat down and simmer for 15 to 20 minutes until tender. Drain and let cool.

Meanwhile, heat the oil in a small skillet over medium-high heat. Add the chorizo and fry for a couple of minutes before adding the panko crumbs. Fry for another 3 to 4 minutes, stirring regularly until the chorizo and panko are all crispy. Transfer to a plate lined with paper towels and let cool slightly.

In a large bowl, toss the potatoes with the mayonnaise, lemon juice, and scallions. Season and add half the chorizo crumb mixture. Toss to coat and serve with extra chorizo crumbs sprinkled on top.

Note: To make this dish gluten free, leave out the panko and add 1 tablespoon of sesame seeds to the salad at the same time as the scallions.

REUBENS

2 ½ tablespoons sauerkraut
2 slices soft rye bread
3 slices salt beef
Canola oil
Dill pickle, to serve

FOR THE RUSSIAN DRESSING
2 tablespoons good-quality
    mayonnaise (check the label
    to make sure it's dairy free)
1 teaspoon tomato ketchup
½ teaspoon horseradish sauce
½ teaspoon Worcestershire
    sauce
¼ teaspoon smoked paprika
2 chives, minced

Serves 1

Reubens are a New York classic. They may be synonymous with Jewish delis but ironically they're not kosher as they usually contain both meat and cheese. I've removed the Swiss cheese but created a DIY Reuben with a smoky Russian dressing that I hope does justice to deli owner Arnold Reuben's original. You can of course add even more beef to make it a true NYC-style sandwich …

Drain the sauerkraut in a fine-mesh colander by pressing down with a wooden spoon to get rid of any excess water, then pat dry between two pieces of paper towels, squeezing to get rid of any more water. For the Russian dressing, whisk together all the ingredients in a small bowl.

Spread a generous amount of the dressing on one slice of the bread. Lay the slices of beef on top and top with the sauerkraut. Spread a thin amount of dressing on the other slice of bread. Spread a little canola oil onto the topside of this slice of bread.

Heat a large, heavy-bottom skillet over medium-high heat. Add the sandwich, oiled side down, and fry for 3 to 4 minutes until the bread is lightly golden. Meanwhile, carefully spread a little more canola oil on the topside of the other slice of bread. Carefully flip over with a spatula and fry for another 2 to 3 minutes.

Slice in half and serve immediately, with a dill pickle on the side.

KHAO SOI WITH BEEF AND RED PEPPER

2 tablespoons peanut,
  sunflower, or canola oil
14 ounces fresh egg noodles
2 round shallots, diced
1 garlic clove, crushed
3/4-inch piece of fresh ginger,
  peeled and finely diced
2 tablespoons red Thai curry
  paste
1 teaspoon curry powder
1 3/4 cups coconut milk
1 3/4 cups beef broth
1 red bell pepper, seeded and
  thinly sliced
2 teaspoons fish sauce
2 teaspoons palm sugar or light
  soft brown sugar
2 thin sirloin steaks (about
  9 ounces in total), sliced into
  1/4-inch-thick strips
1 scallion (white and green
  part), finely sliced
Small handful of fresh cilantro,
  coarsely chopped
Lime wedges, to serve
Sea salt and freshly ground
  black pepper

Serves 4

Khao soi is a street food dish from Northern Thailand, usually made with chicken or beef. This is a slightly simplified version, given that for true *khao soi* you need to make the paste from scratch. If you can find them, pickled mustard greens are a traditional accompaniment.

Heat the oil in large wok or deep, heavy-bottom skillet over medium-high heat. Slice 1 3/4 ounces of the egg noodles into strips 1 1/4 inches long and fry for 2 to 3 minutes until crispy. Transfer to a plate lined with paper towels and season with salt.

Fry the shallots, garlic, and ginger in the same oil (add a little extra if needed) for 2 to 3 minutes until softened. Add the curry paste and powder and cook for another couple of minutes. Add the coconut milk, stock, red pepper, fish sauce, and sugar, stirring well to combine. Bring to a boil, then turn the heat down and simmer for 15 minutes.

Add the rest of the egg noodles to the broth and cook for another 2 minutes. Turn the heat up a little, add the steak slices, and cook until medium rare. Season with salt and pepper.

Divide between bowls and top each with some fried egg noodles, scallion, and cilantro. Serve with lime wedges.

LAMB SHOULDER WITH PUY LENTILS, POMEGRANATE, AND A WARM MINT DRESSING

2 tablespoons pomegranate
   molasses
1 tablespoon canola oil
2 garlic cloves, crushed, plus
   ½ head of garlic, cloves
   separated but unpeeled
1 boneless half shoulder of lamb,
   about 1 ½ pounds
2 bay leaves
Sea salt and freshly ground
   black pepper

FOR THE LENTILS

1 ¼ cups Puy lentils
2 bay leaves
1 large bunch of fresh mint
   leaves, minced
1 teaspoon superfine sugar
½ cup boiling water
1 tablespoon balsamic vinegar
3 tablespoons extra-virgin
   olive oil
Seeds of 1 fresh pomegranate
2 large handfuls of arugula

Serves 4

A guaranteed-to-impress-your-friends dish that is actually a cinch to make. Cover the lamb in a sticky pomegranate molasses glaze and let it roast in the oven while you put your feet up.

Preheat the oven to 350 °F.

Whisk the pomegranate molasses, oil, and crushed garlic together. Cut small, shallow slits in the lamb, then massage the pomegranate-and-oil mixture all over the lamb. Season with salt and pepper.

Place the unpeeled garlic cloves and bay leaves in a small-medium roasting pan. Place the lamb on top and roast for 1 hour and 5 minutes.

Ten minutes before the lamb is due out of the oven, put the lentils and bay leaves in a saucepan and cover with twice the lentils' volume in water. Bring to a boil, then reduce the heat, season, and simmer for 15 to 20 minutes until tender.

Meanwhile, remove the lamb from the oven, cover with foil, and let rest for 10 minutes. To make the dressing, put the chopped mint in a pitcher, add the sugar and boiling water, and stir. When the mixture has cooled slightly, add the vinegar and oil and whisk together briskly to combine.

Drain the lentils. Pour over the warm mint dressing, then season and fold in the pomegranate seeds and arugula. Serve with slices of the lamb on top.

DINNER

BROOKLYN-STYLE PEANUT NOODLES WITH TOFU AND SNOW PEAS

4 ounces soba noodles

2 tablespoons vegetable, sunflower, or peanut oil

7 ounces firm tofu, drained and dried (see page 92), then cut into ¾-inch cubes

3½ ounces pak choi, trimmed and chopped into large pieces

3 ½ ounces snow peas

4 tablespoons crunchy peanut butter

1 tablespoon soy sauce

½ tablespoon rice vinegar

½ teaspoon Sriracha

Juice of ½ lime, plus an extra squeeze to serve

2 tablespoons water

Few drops of sesame oil

1 scallion (white and green parts), sliced on the diagonal

2 teaspoons sesame seeds, to garnish

Serves 2

Another of those hot-plate suppers I used to make in New York —no oven required (because who needs a kitchen with amazing restaurants on every block?). This healthy noodle dish is a riot of textures (tender soba noodles, the crunch of sesame and peanuts, and delicate fried tofu with its crispy coating) and is adapted from a recipe by Jacquie Berger in the excellent *Edible Brooklyn* cookbook, a celebration of that borough's thriving food culture.

Add the noodles to a saucepan of hot water. Bring to a boil and simmer for 3 minutes until al dente. Drain and rinse with cold water.

Meanwhile, heat the oil in a large, heavy-bottom skillet over medium-high heat. Add the tofu and fry until turning crisp and golden on the outside. Add the pak choi and snow peas and stir-fry for another 3 minutes, until the tofu is crisp and the vegetables tender and slightly wilted.

Mix the peanut butter, soy sauce, rice vinegar, Sriracha, and lime juice together to form a thick paste. Thin with the water to make a thick sauce.

Add the peanut sauce and sesame oil to the pan and toss with the vegetables and tofu so they are well coated. Divide the drained noodles between two plates and top with the tofu and vegetables. Serve immediately, topped with scallion and sesame seeds, and a squeeze of lime juice.

CHICKEN PIE

6 skinless, boneless chicken
   thighs
½ onion, diced
2 bay leaves
6 sprigs of fresh thyme
6 peppercorns
1 tablespoon olive oil
5 ¾ ounces smoked bacon
   pieces
1 large leek, trimmed and finely
   sliced
Scant ¼ cup dairy-free
   sunflower spread
⅓ cup all-purpose flour, plus
   extra for dusting
1 ¼ cups chicken broth
Scant ½ cup white wine
1 teaspoon mustard powder
Scant 1 cup oat cream
1 pound, 2 ounces ready-made
   puff pastry (NOT the all-butter
   kind)
1 egg, beaten
Sea salt and freshly ground
   black pepper

Pie dish, approximately
   12 x 10 inches (or 9½ inches
   if round), lightly greased

Serves 4

Cut into the golden flaky crust of this pie and underneath you'll find tender chunks of chicken thighs, smoky bacon, leeks, and a rich white-wine sauce. It's what winter nights are begging for ... (See photograph on page 68.)

Place the chicken thighs in a large saucepan with the onion, bay leaves, 3 of the thyme sprigs, and the peppercorns. Cover with water and bring to a boil. Turn the heat down, cover, and poach at a gentle simmer for 15 minutes, or until the chicken is cooked through. Discard the water and herbs and transfer the chicken to a plate lined with paper towels.

Heat the oil in a large saucepan over medium heat and add the bacon pieces and the leaves from the remaining thyme sprigs. Fry for 3 to 4 minutes until the bacon pieces are crisp and cooked through. Move to one side of the pan and add the leek. Fry over low-medium heat for 5 to 6 minutes, until softened.

Meanwhile, melt the dairy-free spread in a separate saucepan over low-medium heat, then add the flour, stirring continuously until you have a smooth, golden roux. Pour in the chicken broth, increase the heat until the broth is simmering, and keep whisking until it is all incorporated into the roux. Stir in the wine, then the mustard powder and oat cream. Simmer for 2 to 3 minutes then remove from the heat.

Cut the chicken into large chunks. Pour the sauce into the pan with the bacon and leeks. Add the chicken pieces and stir to combine. Season, pour into the pie dish, and let cool. Meanwhile, preheat the oven to 400 °F.

Lightly dust a counter and rolling pin with flour, then roll out the pastry to about ¼ inch thick. Brush the rim of the pie dish with a little beaten egg. Lift up the pastry using your rolling pin, then drape it over the dish. Trim the edges, leaving ¾ inch pastry over the sides of the dish, then press down and crimp all the way around the edge with your fingertips. Brush the top of the pie with the rest of the beaten egg, then prick a few holes in the center of the pastry with a fork.

Bake for 35 to 40 minutes, until the top is golden.

CURRY NIGHT

1. SAAG/PALAK "PANEER"

2 ½ tablespoons vegetable oil
7 ounces firm tofu, drained and
    dried (see page 92), then cut
    into ¾-inch cubes
14 ounces baby leaf spinach
2 round shallots, finely diced
Thumb-size piece of ginger,
    peeled and minced
1 garlic clove, minced
1 teaspoon ground coriander
½ teaspoon ground cumin
½ teaspoon garam masala
½ teaspoon cayenne pepper
4 tablespoons water
Scant ¼ cup coconut milk
Sea salt

*Serves 2 as a main dish or 4 as
a side*

Saag panéer is made with puréed spinach and cubes of firm, mild paneer cheese. It's also known as *palak paneer* as the dish originates from the Punjab where *palak* means spinach (*saag* can refer to other leafy greens). Either way, it's delicious but no friend of the dairy free. Luckily, firm tofu is a good substitute for paneer, having a similar texture. Fry it first to get it golden and crisp on the outside.

Heat 2 tablespoons of the oil in a heavy-bottom skillet over medium-high heat. Add the tofu and fry until golden, for about 10 minutes. Transfer the tofu to a plate lined with paper towels.

Meanwhile, cook the spinach in a pan of boiling water until wilted, for about 3 minutes. Drain well and then purée in a food processor. Leave to one side.

Return the skillet that you cooked the tofu in to medium heat and add the remaining ½ tablespoon of oil. Add the shallots and fry for a few minutes until softened. Add the ginger and garlic and fry for another 1 minute. Add the ground spices and fry for about 1 minute, stirring with a wooden spoon, just until they have released their fragrance.

Add the puréed spinach and the water. Bring to a boil, then simmer for about 3 minutes. Stir the tofu into the mixture before adding the coconut milk and stirring again. Cook for 2 more minutes until the tofu is piping hot. Add salt to taste and serve immediately.

2. TANDOORI CHICKEN

2 chicken legs (about 10 ounces
    each)
Good pinch of sea salt
Juice of 1 ½ lemons
Scant ½ cup coconut yogurt
½ tablespoon vegetable oil
2 teaspoons tandoori masala
    powder
½ teaspoon cayenne pepper

Serves 2

Fire-engine red tandoori chicken is a curry-house staple. Marinated in yogurt and tandoori spices, it is then blasted in a tandoor oven. While you won't match the furnace heat of the tandoor, nor the ruby hue at home, you can make this delicious approximation with coconut yogurt and a hot oven.

Use a sharp knife to make two deep cuts down the middle of the top side of the chicken legs (the side with most of the meat on it). Put into a baking dish and sprinkle with salt. Pour two-thirds of the lemon juice over the top and rub into the meat. Set aside for 10 minutes.

Mix together the coconut yogurt, the remaining lemon juice, and the oil in a large bowl. Stir in the tandoori masala powder and cayenne pepper to make a smooth paste. Pour any lemon juice from the bottom of the dish with the chicken into the marinade and stir to combine. Pour this over the chicken legs, turning to make sure they are well-coated all over. Cover with plastic wrap and marinate in the refrigerator for at least 8 hours or overnight.

When ready to cook, preheat the oven to 450 °F. Transfer the chicken legs to another baking dish, shaking off any excess marinade. Cook for 25 minutes or until the chicken juices run clear. Serve with brown rice and fresh naan breads.

3. CHERRY RAITA

½ cup coconut yogurt
1 garlic clove, crushed
1 tablespoon lemon juice
1 ¾ ounces ripe cherries
    (about 6), pitted and
    finely sliced
Small handful of fresh mint,
    minced
Sea salt and freshly ground
    black pepper

Serves 4

A luscious, creamy raita with slivers of cherries and fresh mint ...

Whisk the yogurt, crushed garlic, and lemon juice together until you have a thick sauce. Fold in the cherry slices and mint. Season to taste.

CONFIT DUCK LEGS WITH CARROT AND ORANGE PURÉE

1 tablespoon sea salt
2 duck legs
Small handful of fresh thyme
    sprigs
2 garlic cloves, thinly sliced
About 12 ounces duck fat

FOR THE PURÉE
14 ounces carrots, peeled and
    diced
Finely grated zest of ½ orange
    and 1 tablespoon juice
1 garlic clove, crushed
2 ½ tablespoons extra-virgin
    olive oil
Fresh thyme leaves, to sprinkle
Sea salt and freshly ground
    black pepper

Serves 2

This impressive-looking duck dish is actually a cinch to make. It's inspired by a tapa I ate in Seville of crispy, salty duck with pumpkin purée. At the time, Seville's famous orange trees were in full bloom, which inspired me to recreate the dish with oranges and carrots for a shot of sunshine on the plate.

The night before you want to make the dish, rub the salt all over the duck legs, then sprinkle some of the thyme and garlic over the bottom of a shallow baking dish. Place the duck legs in the dish, then sprinkle the rest of the thyme and garlic on top. Cover and chill overnight.

The next day, preheat the oven to 300 °F. Remove the duck from the refrigerator and pat dry with paper towels, removing some but not all of the salt.

Transfer the garlic and thyme to a medium-size Dutch oven and nestle the duck legs on top. Melt the duck fat in a saucepan over low heat and then pour it over the top of the duck legs until they are completely covered. The exact amount will depend on the dimensions of your Dutch oven, but if you find yourself slightly short of duck fat, top it off with vegetable or sunflower oil.

Cover and cook in the oven for 2½ hours or until very tender. Remove from the oven. (If not using immediately, the cooled duck confit will keep, covered in the fat, in an airtight container in the refrigerator for a couple of weeks.)

Turn the oven up to 400 °F. To crisp up the duck legs, remove them from the fat and place in a shallow baking dish, skin side up. Roast for 25 minutes, or until the skin is golden and crispy.

Make the carrot purée 20 minutes before the duck is ready to serve. Steam or boil the carrots in a large saucepan until tender. Drain, setting aside 2 tablespoons of the cooking water, then return the carrots to the pan off the heat, adding back the reserved water. Add the orange zest and juice, and the crushed garlic. Stir to combine, then pour in the oil. Blitz with a stick blender until smooth and creamy, then season generously.

Serve each duck leg on top of some purée and sprinkle thyme leaves over the top. Serve with broccoli and a good bottle of red.

TARATOR CHICKEN IN PROSCIUTTO WITH WALNUT, GRAPE, AND RADICCHIO SALAD

1½ cups walnut pieces

6 skinless, boneless chicken breasts

1⅓ cups white bread crumbs

1 garlic clove, peeled

Large handful of fresh tarragon (about ¾ ounces), coarsely chopped

Large handful of flat-leaf parsley (about 1 ounce), coarsely chopped

1 tablespoon red wine vinegar

⅔ cup water

Scant ¼- ½ cup extra-virgin olive oil, plus extra for drizzling

12 slices prosciutto

Sea salt and freshly ground black pepper

FOR THE SALAD

2 tablespoons extra-virgin olive oil

2 teaspoons red wine vinegar

1 teaspoon superfine sugar

5 ½ ounces red grapes, halved lengthwise

7 ounces radicchio or red chicory, finely shredded (substitute white chicory if red is out of season)

Small handful of fresh tarragon leaves, chopped

Serves 6

Tarator means different things in different Eastern European and Middle Eastern countries, but in Turkey it refers to a thick sauce made with bread crumbs, walnuts, and herbs. I first came across it in Sally Butcher's excellent *Persia in Peckham* and thought it would make a delicious stuffing for chicken breasts wrapped in prosciutto (that aughts dinner-party staple—so often made with a creamy cheese). The recipe for the *tarator* is adapted from Butcher's.

Toast the walnut pieces in a small, dry skillet over medium heat until golden. Keep a careful eye on them as they can burn quickly. Tip onto a plate, let cool, then chop. Preheat the oven to 400 °F.

Cut along one side of each chicken breast—almost but not all the way through—so it opens out like a book.

Put the bread crumbs, 1 cup of the chopped walnuts (set aside the remainder for the salad), garlic, tarragon, and parsley in a food processor and whizz to combine. Pour in the vinegar and water. Whizz briefly; then, with the processor running, pour in the oil in a very slow, steady trickle until you have a thick but wet paste (coarse, but with a similar consistency to hummus). Remove from the processor and season generously.

Fold the chicken breasts out on a cutting board and place a couple of spoonfuls of the *tarator* inside the middle of one half of the opened chicken breast, spreading it along the inside. Close the other half of the chicken breast on top of the mixture. Wrap each chicken breast in two slices of prosciutto, overlapping each other, with the ends of the ham tucked underneath the chicken breast.

Space the chicken breasts out in a roasting pan and drizzle a little oil over the top. Bake for 25 minutes until the prosciutto is crisp, the chicken is cooked through, and its juices run clear.

Meanwhile, to make the salad, whisk the oil, vinegar, and sugar together to combine. Toss this dressing with the grape halves, reserved toasted, chopped walnuts, shredded radicchio, and most of the tarragon leaves, in a large bowl. Garnish with the rest of the tarragon leaves and divide between serving plates. Serve with the chicken to one side.

DAUPHINOISE POTATOES

2 tablespoons dairy-free
    sunflower spread,
    plus extra for greasing
1 pound, 7 ounces Desirée
    potatoes, peeled
Scant 1 cup almond milk
2 tablespoons all-purpose flour
1 ½ teaspoons mustard powder
2 large garlic cloves, crushed
1 cup oat cream
½ teaspoon ground nutmeg
Sea salt and freshly ground
    black pepper

Serves 6

Creamy layers of potatoes drowning in cream and cheese—I must admit, I wasn't optimistic about recreating Dauphinoise potatoes. But, after a couple of trial runs, I've cracked it. The trick is to make a white sauce instead of just adding dairy-free milk and oat cream to the potatoes (they'll split if you do), and to give it a little *umami* kick with mustard powder. Broil it for 5 minutes at the end and the result is a golden Dauphinoise you'll be proud to serve to the most committed dairy-eater.

Preheat the oven to 320 °F. Grease a medium-size gratin or other ovenproof dish with dairy-free spread. Slice the potatoes (or carefully use a mandolin) into ⅛-inch slices.

Put the almond milk in a saucepan, season with a little salt, and bring to a boil, then turn down to a simmer.

Meanwhile, melt the dairy-free spread in a separate saucepan over low-medium heat, then add the flour, stirring until you have a smooth roux. Pour the almond milk onto the roux, whisking until all the milk is incorporated. Stir in the mustard powder and garlic and simmer for 2 minutes, before adding the oat cream. Simmer for another 2 to 3 minutes, then adjust the seasoning and remove from the heat.

Arrange the potato slices in layers in the baking dish. Pour the sauce all over them, making sure the potatoes are well covered in the sauce. Use a small fine-mesh strainer to sprinkle the nutmeg over the top of the potatoes.

Bake on the middle shelf in the oven for 1 hour, until the potatoes are tender. Preheat the broiler just before they are ready, then broil for 5 minutes, or until the top has lots of enticing golden patches.

AMERICAN BARBECUE NIGHT

1. "BUTTERMILK" ROASTED CHICKEN

1 tablespoon lemon juice
1 ¼ cups almond milk
2 teaspoons plain soy yogurt
3 teaspoons cayenne pepper
3 teaspoons mustard powder
4 garlic cloves, peeled and
    bashed with the flat of a knife
2 teaspoons sea salt and plenty
    of freshly ground black pepper
2 teaspoons maple syrup
2 ¼ pounds chicken thighs and
    drumsticks
Olive oil

Serves 4

What if you could get the tenderness of fried chicken without all the deep-fried grease? Enter "buttermilk" roasted chicken, adapted from a Nigella Lawson recipe. Thighs and drumsticks (so much more flavorsome than chicken breasts) get a long marinating in garlic, spices, and a dairy-free "buttermilk"—the result is chicken with burnished-gold skin and succulent meat. No deep-frying required. The perfect accompaniments have to be cornbread and slaw (see pages 80-81).

Add the lemon juice to the almond milk, stir, let rest for 5 minutes, then stir in the soy yogurt.

To make the marinade, add the cayenne pepper, mustard powder, bashed garlic cloves, salt, pepper, and maple syrup to the almond "buttermilk," whisking briskly with a fork to combine.

Place the chicken thighs and drumsticks in a large, sealable freezer bag. Pour in the marinade, seal, and place flat in a baking dish in the refrigerator, making sure the chicken is well coated. Marinate in the refrigerator for at least 6 hours or overnight.

Preheat the oven to 425 °F. Remove the chicken from the marinade and shake off any excess liquid. Space the chicken pieces out in a roasting pan, drizzle with a little oil and roast for 30 minutes, until the chicken is cooked through and the skin is golden brown with dark, burnished patches.

2. RED CABBAGE AND SESAME SLAW

Scant ¼ cup lemon juice
Scant ¼ cup white wine vinegar
1 tablespoon superfine sugar
1 red cabbage, finely shredded
1 scallion (white and green
     part), sliced
Large handful of cilantro
     leaves
1 tablespoon sesame seeds
Sea salt and freshly ground
     black pepper

Serves 6 to 8

A peppy slaw to serve at a barbecue, with "buttermilk" chicken (see page 78) or pulled pork and ribs. Calcium-rich sesame seeds add texture and crunch, while cilantro and lemon juice add freshness and zest, meaning there's no need for mayo.

Whisk together the lemon juice, vinegar, and sugar. Pour this mixture over the shredded cabbage and stir to combine.

Add the scallion, cilantro, and sesame seeds. Season and toss everything together well.

3. DAIRY-FREE CORNBREAD

1 ½ cups soy or almond milk
Juice of ½ lemon
1 ⅔ cups cornmeal
¼ cup self-rising flour, sifted
1 teaspoon baking powder
½ teaspoon baking soda
¼ cup superfine sugar
1 teaspoon sea salt
1 large egg, beaten
2 tablespoons dairy-free
    sunflower spread,
    melted and cooled
1 scallion (white and green
    part), finely sliced

8 x 8-inch square baking pan,
    greased and lined

Makes 16 squares/Serves 8

There's something comforting about cornbread. It's that golden crust combined with the soft, primrose-yellow base. This sweet staple of the American South is basically cake you can get away with eating with savory dishes—serve it with a deep-red, smoky chiei, or with the "buttermilk" chicken (see page 78) and red cabbage and sesame slaw opposite.

Preheat the oven to 400 °F.

Mix together the soy or almond milk and lemon juice in a measuring cup and let stand for 5 minutes.

Meanwhile, fold all the dry ingredients together in a large bowl with a large metal spoon, until just combined. Pour in the almond milk and lemon juice mixture; add the egg, melted spread, and scallion and whisk together to combine.

Pour the batter into the prepared pan and bake for 25 minutes, or until golden on top. Let cool for 5 minutes in the pan, before cutting into squares and turning out onto a wire rack to cool slightly. Best served when still warm.

VIETNAMESE CHICKEN AND PUMPKIN CURRY

2 lemongrass stalks, peeled and
   finely sliced
3 garlic cloves, minced
1 tablespoon sunflower or
   vegetable oil
2 round shallots, finely diced
2 tablespoons curry powder
1 teaspoon ground turmeric
1 pound skinless, boneless
   chicken thighs, diced
1 3/4 cups chicken broth
9 ounces pumpkin or butternut
   squash, seeded and cut
   into 3/4-inch cubes
7 ounces potatoes, peeled and
   cut into 3/4-inch cubes
1 cup coconut milk
3 teaspoons sugar
2 tablespoons fish sauce
Fresh cilantro leaves,
   to garnish
Red chile, sliced, to garnish
   (optional)
Sea salt and freshly ground
   black pepper

Serves 4

Vietnamese curry is so creamy and satisfying, it's hard to believe it's not laced with dairy. I developed a minor addiction to it on my honeymoon in Vietnam, where the chef at our hotel gave me his recipe after I kept ordering it. After playing around with the dish back home, this is my version—the sweet pumpkin or squash makes a great foil for the *umami*-rich broth. Vietnamese curry is often served with a crisp baguette, but also works well with white or brown rice.

Blitz the lemongrass and garlic in a small food processor or mini chopper to form a thick paste.

Heat a large, heavy-bottom saucepan over medium heat. Add the oil, then fry the shallots for about 4 minutes, until softened. Add the lemongrass and garlic paste and fry for 2 minutes, until fragrant. Stir the curry powder and turmeric into the mixture and fry for just 30 seconds, then add the diced chicken. Fry for a couple of minutes until the chicken is coated in the spices and starting to brown, then pour in the broth.

Bring the broth to a boil, then add the diced pumpkin or squash and the potatoes. Reduce the heat slightly, season, cover, and simmer for 10 minutes.

Add the coconut milk, sugar, and fish sauce. Simmer, uncovered, over medium-high heat for another 5 minutes. Check to ensure chicken is cooked through and check the seasoning.

Garnish with the cilantro leaves, and slices of red chile if desired, and serve with lime wedges.

TOAD IN THE HOLE

1 ½ teaspoons fresh thyme
   leaves
1 cup soy milk
¾ cup all-purpose flour
1 teaspoon salt
2 large eggs
2 ½ tablespoons vegetable or
   sunflower oil
8 good-quality, herby pork
   sausages (around 1 pound, and
   check the label to make sure
   they're dairy free)

Large roasting pan,
   approx. 14 x 12 inches

Serves 4

When I was a kid, toad in the hole was a fixture on my "top ten dinners" list (as were fish fingers; I was quite the junior gourmand). Even now, there's something about that combination of sausages surrounded by golden, puffy Yorkshire pudding batter that brings back the comforts of a childhood dinner. My dairy-free twist is to infuse fresh and fragrant thyme leaves in soy milk for 20 minutes before whisking. You'll really notice the difference in the flavor of the batter, and no one will guess it's made with soy if you don't want them to.

Add the thyme leaves to the soy milk. Stir once and let steep for 20 minutes.

Sift the flour and salt into a large bowl. Make a well in the center and crack in the eggs.

Pour in the thyme-infused soy milk slowly, about one-third at a time, whisking after each addition until all the milk is added and the batter is smooth with no lumps. Let stand for around 20 minutes. Meanwhile, preheat the oven to 425 °F.

Heat ½ tablespoon of the oil in a large skillet. Add the sausages and fry until browned all over. Pour the remaining 2 tablespoons of oil into the large roasting pan and place in the hot oven for 5 to 10 minutes until the oil is smoking.

Remove the pan from the oven and add the sausages, evenly spacing them. Pour in the batter and immediately return to the oven. Cook for 20 to 25 minutes until the batter is golden and puffed up and the sausages are cooked through. Don't be tempted to open the oven door during cooking as this may cause the batter to sink.

FOR YORKSHIRE PUDDING *Serves 4 to 6*
Follow the recipe for the batter, as above, but cook in a 12-section muffin tray, with a little heated oil in each section and dividing the batter equally between the holes. Bake for 20 minutes, until golden and puffy.

BANGERS AND OLIVE OIL MASH

8 good-quality pork sausages
(check the label to make sure
they're dairy free)
2 ¼ pounds mealy potatoes,
peeled and cubed
4 tablespoons extra-virgin
olive oil
3 tablespoons almond milk
Sea salt and freshly ground
black pepper

Serves 4

Big fluffy clouds of mash don't have to be made with dollops of butter. Olive oil mash is buttery mash's more sophisticated cousin—there's a slight, pleasing hint of extra-virgin olive oil that pairs well with most meat dishes, and the mash is every bit as light and creamy as its buttery relative.

Fry, bake, or broil the sausages according to your preference.

Place the potatoes in a large pan of cold, salted water. Bring to a boil, then turn the heat down and simmer for about 15 minutes, until tender.

Drain the potatoes and leave in the colander for a few minutes to dry out a bit. Return to the warm pan and pour in the oil. Mash vigorously with a potato masher until lump free, soft, and fluffy. Season, then stir in the almond milk and mash again.

Serve immediately with the sausages. I'm always temped to stick the sausages into a mash mountain, in the manner of *The Beano* comic. Steamed broccoli works as a side dish if you're feeling virtuous (but Dennis the Menace wouldn't approve).

MOJITO SALMON WITH PLANTAIN FRIES

FOR THE SALMON

3 tablespoons stale white
    bread crumbs or panko
    bread crumbs
2 teaspoons mint leaves
Finely grated zest of 1 lime
½ teaspoon sea salt
Good grinding of freshly ground
    black pepper
2 salmon fillets
1 tablespoon olive oil
2 teaspoons rum

FOR THE FRIES

1¼ cups vegetable, sunflower, or
    canola oil
1 plantain, still a little green but
    not completely unripe, peeled
    and cut into evenly size fries,
    about 2¾ inches long
Sea salt

FOR THE MAYO

Juice of ½ lime
1 teaspoon mint leaves
1½ teaspoons Sriracha or
    hot sauce
5 tablespoons good-quality
    mayonnaise (check it's
    dairy free)

Serves 2

In South London, where I lived for many years, the streets are paved with plantains. You'll spot them everywhere, in crates stacked three deep outside West Indian stores. To the untrained eye they look like overgrown bananas, but plantains are much starchier and firmer than their sweeter cousins. For a taste of the tropics on a gray, rainy day, I make this easy dinner of mojito salmon served with plantain fries and a fiery mint and lime mayo. As for the salmon—it's having its own private carnival in the oven with lime, mint, and a little rum over crisp bread crumbs.

Preheat the oven to 375 °F and line a baking dish with foil or parchment paper.

Mix together the bread crumbs, mint, lime zest, salt, and pepper on a plate and press the salmon flesh side down into the mixture. Turn the fillets back the right way and place in the baking dish. Sprinkle any remaining bread crumb mix from the plate over the fillets so they have an even-ish topping of crumbs.

Warm the olive oil in a small skillet over medium heat. Remove the pan from the heat (vital if you'd like your eyebrows to remain where they are) and pour in the rum. Return to the heat and melt until the oil and rum are starting to bubble and turn a light golden brown.

Pour the rum mix over the salmon fillets, put in the oven, and bake for about 10 to 12 minutes until the salmon is just cooked through. Turn the broiler to high and then broil for about 2 minutes, or until the topping is crisp and golden.

Meanwhile, heat the vegetable oil for the fries in a large, heavy-bottom skillet. Once the oil is very hot and starting to smoke, add the plantain and fry for about 3 to 4 minutes, or until golden brown and tender in the middle. Do this in two batches if necessary, so as not to overcrowd the pan. Take off the heat and transfer the fries with a slotted spoon or kitchen tongs to a plate lined with a few sheets of paper towels to absorb the excess oil. Season with salt.

To make the mayo, put all the ingredients into a bowl and whisk briskly with a fork to combine. Check the seasoning and add a little more Sriracha or hot sauce if required. Serve the salmon with the plantain fries, and a simple watercress salad, if desired.

GRIDDLED LAMB STEAKS WITH CIDER GRAVY AND CANNELLINI BEAN AND HERB MASH

2 lamb steaks (about 5½ ounces each) or 4 small lamb leg steaks
1 tablespoon vegetable or olive oil
1¼ cups medium-hard cider
1 tablespoon soy sauce
1½ tablespoons cornstarch
2½ tablespoons cold water
Sea salt and freshly ground black pepper

FOR THE BEANS
½ cup dried cannellini beans
3 cups cold water
½ teaspoon baking soda
1½ tablespoons olive oil
1 garlic clove, crushed
Needles from 2 sprigs of fresh rosemary
Leaves from 3 sprigs of fresh thyme

Serves 2

I love chops, but you don't exactly get a lot of juicy, delicious lamb for your buck. For around the same price, you can pick up a pair of lamb steaks: all meat, no bones. Here I've paired them with cannellini bean and rosemary mash, a traditional Tuscan dish. If you're in a hurry, use a can of cannellini beans instead, but patience pays off–dried ones soaked overnight make a much softer, creamier mash. Apples and cider are best known for partnering up with pork, but they also make a delicious compadre for lamb. Though, obviously, this gravy will work really well with pork chops or sausages, too.

Place the cannellini beans in a large bowl, cover with the water, add the baking soda, and stir to dissolve. Let soak overnight or for a minimum of 6 hours.

Drain and rinse the beans. Place in a large, heavy-bottom saucepan and cover with 3 cups cold water. Bring to a boil and boil rapidly for 10 minutes. Turn the heat down, cover, and simmer for about 1 hour and 20 minutes or until soft and tender. Check the beans regularly, adding more water if necessary. Drain and set aside while you cook the lamb.

Brush both sides of the lamb steaks with a little oil and season with salt and pepper. Heat a griddle or heavy-bottom skillet to high and fry for around 3 to 4 minutes on each side, depending on the thickness of the steaks and how pink you like them. After frying the first side, use kitchen tongs to brown the fat on the side of each steak. Transfer the steaks to two dinner plates and cover with foil to keep them warm.

Heat the oil for the beans in a saucepan over medium heat and fry the garlic and herbs for 2 minutes. Add the drained beans and heat until piping hot, 1 to 2 minutes, stirring with a wooden spoon and using it to crush and gently mash the beans, which should still retain some texture. Season liberally with salt and divide between the two plates.

Return the lamb pan to the heat. Pour in the cider and swirl to deglaze the pan. If you used a griddle, decant the mixture into another saucepan. Add the soy sauce, bring to a boil, and simmer for 2 to 3 minutes. Mix the cornstarch and water together, then stir into the gravy. Cook for 3 to 4 minutes, stirring constantly. Pour over the lamb and serve with broccoli, savoy cabbage, or collards.

CHORIZO, CANNELLINI BEAN, AND ARUGULA STIR-FRY

½ tablespoon olive oil
1 red chile, seeded and finely diced
2 scallions, finely sliced and separated into white and green slices
1 (4-ounce) piece chorizo, cut into ½-inch slices
14-ounce can cannellini beans, rinsed and drained
1 ½ tablespoons balsamic vinegar
2 ¾ ounces arugula
Sourdough bread, sliced, to serve

Serves 2 as a light lunch or supper

Who says stir-fries have to have Asian ingredients? This Spanish-ish dish is one of my absolute favorite standbys on those nights when you're late back from work and just want some comfort food in a bowl in front of Netflix. It also makes a delicious lunchbox the next day and can easily be doubled.

Heat the oil in a large, heavy-bottom skillet over medium-high heat. Add the chile and white slices of scallion and sizzle for about 1 minute.

Add the chorizo and turn the heat up to high. Fry for about 3 minutes or until cooked through and turning crispy around the edges.

Stir in the cannellini beans and cover in all those lovely orange oils released from the chorizo. Stir-fry for around 2 minutes. Pour in the balsamic vinegar and add the arugula. Stir for around 20 seconds, just until slightly wilted.

Top with the green scallion slices and serve immediately with some sourdough bread.

SHRIMP RISOTTO

2 tablespoons olive oil
1 onion, finely diced
2 garlic cloves, crushed
2 stalks of celery, trimmed and
    very finely sliced
1 ⅓ cups Arborio risotto rice
1 cup dry white wine
3 cups hot fish (or chicken) broth
6 ½ ounces raw king shrimp
1 ⅓ cups frozen peas
1 scallion (white and green
    part), finely sliced on the
    diagonal
Finely grated zest of ½ lemon
1 ½ teaspoons minced mint
Swirl of extra-virgin olive oil
Sea salt and freshly ground
    black pepper

Serves 4

Don't be wary about making risotto—it's not complicated, just methodical. There's something meditative about standing at the stove, stirring with your wooden spoon, while the grains of rice grow fat on wine and broth. The reward for your patience is a creamy risotto with plump shrimp and the zesty, sunny flavors of peas, mint, and lemon ...

Heat the oil in a deep, heavy-bottom saucepan or ovenproof Dutch oven over low-medium heat. Fry the onion, garlic, and celery gently for 10 minutes until softened. Turn the heat up a little, add the rice, and stir to coat in the oil and vegetables. Fry for 1 minute, then pour in the wine and simmer for 1 minute.

Turn the heat down to low-medium again and add a ladleful of broth. Stir with a wooden spoon until the rice has absorbed the broth. Repeat, adding a ladleful at a time and stirring, while it absorbs, until you have added all the broth and the rice grains are plump and tender. Season generously.

Stir in the shrimp and peas and cook for 2 minutes, then cover and cook for another 2 minutes until the shrimp are cooked through. Stir in the scallion, most of the lemon zest, and 1 teaspoon of the mint; add the extra-virgin olive oil, then remove from the heat and let stand with the lid on for a couple of minutes. Check the seasoning, garnish with the remaining mint and lemon zest, and serve.

SALT AND PEPPER TOFU

14 ounces firm tofu
1 cup cornstarch
½ tablespoon sea salt
⅔ cup peanut, vegetable,
    or sunflower oil, plus
    ½ tablespoon
2 garlic cloves, finely sliced
1 red chile, seeded and diced
1 to 2 scallions (white and
    green parts), sliced
Soy sauce, for drizzling
Freshly ground black pepper

*Serves 2 as a main dish or 4 as
an appetizer*

Salt and pepper tofu is one of *those* dishes—if it's on the menu, I have to order it. It's something about the combination of the delicate, mild tofu inside and the crunchy, peppery coating—not to mention all those chiles and garlic. It's easy to make at home, too—just allow plenty of time to drain the tofu before you start frying.

Drain the tofu an hour or so ahead of time by wrapping it in paper towels, then in a clean dish towel. Put it in a colander in the sink, then place a heavy object on top and let drain. Pat dry and cut into 1¼-inch cubes.

Combine the cornstrach, salt, and plenty of black pepper in a large bowl. Add the tofu and toss gently to coat.

Heat the ⅔ cup oil in a large, heavy-bottom skillet over high heat until sizzling. Test whether the oil is hot enough by adding one tofu cube—it should start sizzling straight away. Working in batches, fry the tofu on one side for a couple of minutes until golden, then use kitchen tongs to carefully turn on its sides to brown all over. Transfer to a plate lined with paper towels.

Meanwhile, heat the remaining ½ tablespoon oil in a small skillet over medium-high heat. Fry the garlic and chile for 1 to 2 minutes until the garlic starts to color. Throw the tofu cubes back in the pan briefly with the scallion and toss to mix. Arrange on the plates and drizzle soy sauce over the top to serve.

Serve on its own as an appetizer, or as a main course with rice and broccoli, stir-fried with soy and garlic.

CREAMY SWEET POTATO, BACON, AND THYME PASTA

14 ounces dried orecchiette or
conchiglie pasta
2 tablespoons olive oil
10 ½ ounces sweet potato, cut
into ¾-inch cubes
3 ounces small bacon pieces
1 garlic clove, crushed
½ teaspoon ground nutmeg
Leaves from 2 sprigs of fresh
thyme
⅔ cup oat cream
Small handful of flat-leaf parsley,
chopped
Sea salt and freshly ground
black pepper

Serves 4

Creamy pasta needn't belong on your banned list. Make this easy and filling pasta with sweet potato, crisp cubes of bacon, and fresh herbs one of your weeknight staples ...

Cook the pasta in a pan of salted, boiling water until al dente. Drain, setting aside 2 tablespoons of the cooking water.

Meanwhile, heat the oil in a large, heavy-bottom skillet over medium-high heat and fry the sweet potato for 5 minutes until starting to turn golden. Add the bacon and fry for another 1 to 2 minutes before adding the garlic, nutmeg, and thyme. Fry for another minute, then remove from the heat.

Return the pasta to its pan with the contents of the skillet. Pour in the oat cream and stir to coat the pasta. Season and add a little of the reserved cooking water to thin the sauce.

Stir in the parsley and serve immediately.

PANCETTA, ZUCCHINI, AND TOMATO CARBONARA

1 tablespoon olive oil
2 garlic cloves, crushed
7 ounces cubetti de pancetta
1 large zucchini (about
    10½ ounces), cut into
    ½-inch cubes
1 pound, 2 ounces dried spaghetti
3 eggs, plus 1 egg yolk
10 ½ ounces medium vine
    tomatoes, halved, seeded, and
    cut into ½-inch cubes
Sea salt and freshly ground
    black pepper

Serves 4 (very hungry people)

The idea for this comes from a restaurant somewhere in the backstreets of Rome. I can't remember the restaurant's name (it's somewhere in Trastevere and the décor is a bit garish), but I'll never forget their sublime carbonara, studded with garlicky zucchini and tender tomatoes. I first ate it in my pre-dairy-free days, but luckily a bit of a tinker around proves it's just as delicious without mountains of Parmesan.

Heat the oil in a skillet over medium heat. Add the garlic and cook for 1 to 2 minutes before adding the pancetta. Fry for 3 to 4 minutes until starting to crisp up, before adding the diced zucchini. Cook for another 3 minutes until the zucchini cubes are tender, then remove from the heat.

Meanwhile, cook the spaghetti in a pan of boiling, well-salted water, until al dente. Beat the eggs and yolk together in a bowl, season generously with black pepper, and place to one side.

When the spaghetti is cooked, remove 2 tablespoons of the cooking water and place to one side in a small cup or mug. Drain the rest of the pasta and return to the pan. Add the zucchini, pancetta, and oil from the skillet and toss well, then stir in the diced tomatoes.

Remove from the heat and pour in the beaten eggs, stirring quickly as you do so to coat all the spaghetti strands. Add the reserved cooking water, a little at a time and only if needed, to loosen the sauce slightly. Season with salt and more pepper, to taste. Eat straight away.

FISH PIE

FOR THE MASHED POTATO TOPPING

2 ¼ pounds mealy potatoes, cubed
4 tablespoons light olive oil
3 tablespoons almond milk
2 teaspoons panko bread crumbs (optional)
Sea salt and freshly ground black pepper

FOR THE FILLING

½ onion, minced
1 bay leaf
6 black peppercorns
2 cloves
1 pound, 7 ounces fresh fish fillets, a mixture of sustainably sourced smoked haddock, salmon, and white fish, such as cod, deboned, skinned and diced
2 cups soy or almond milk
3 ½ ounces raw, peeled king shrimp
4 tablespons dairy-free sunflower spread
⅓ cup all-purpose flour
2 teaspoons mustard powder
1 cup oat cream
Small handful of flat-leaf parsley, minced

Baking dish, approximately 11 x 8½ inches

Serves 4 to 6

Fish pie is a duvet of a dinner—so cozy and warming you just want to burrow into it. No wonder it never really goes out of fashion. This version is every bit as good as milk-laden versions: a rich, creamy sauce, tender flaked fish, and a layer of fluffy mash on top.

Place the potatoes in a large pan of cold, salted water. Bring to a boil, then turn the heat down and simmer for around 15 minutes until tender. Drain and leave in the colander for a few minutes to dry out a bit, then return them to the warm pan and pour in the oil. Mash vigorously with a potato masher until lump free, soft, and fluffy. Season, then stir in the almond milk and mash again.

Preheat the oven to 400 °F.

Meanwhile, put the onion, bay leaf, peppercorns, cloves, and fish (not the shrimp) into a large pan and pour in the soy or almond milk. Bring to a gentle boil, then poach the fish at a gentle simmer for 5 minutes. Add the shrimp and continue to simmer for another 2 to 3 minutes, until the fish and shrimp are cooked through.

Using a spatula, transfer the fish, shrimp, and onions to the baking dish, making a layer of fish on the bottom of the dish. Set the infused milk to one side.

Melt the dairy-free spread in a clean pan over low-medium heat, then add the flour, stirring continuously until you have a smooth roux. Place a strainer above the roux and strain the milk mixture through it, discarding the bay and spices. Whisk until all the milk is incorporated into the roux. Stir in the mustard powder, before adding the oat cream. Simmer for another 2 to 3 minutes then remove from the heat, add salt and pepper to taste, stir in the chopped parsley, and then pour over the fish.

Top with the mashed potato, using a fork to fluff the top. Sprinkle the panko bread crumbs over the top, if using, and bake for 30 to 35 minutes until the peaks of the mashed potato, and the bread crumbs if using, are golden. Serve immediately.

TOASTED WALNUT PESTO

Scant ¾ cup walnut pieces
Scant ¼ cup cashews, chopped
    into small pieces
1 small garlic clove, peeled
Bunch of flat-leaf parsley
    (1 ounce)
Bunch of basil (1 ounce)
Scant ½ cup extra-virgin olive oil
Sea salt

Makes 1 jar

This versatile pesto tastes great tossed through pasta and gnocchi or on top of baked chicken and fish. The creamy cashews temper the earthy flavor of the walnuts and mean there's no need for Parmesan.

Toast the walnuts in a dry skillet over medium heat until they start turning golden. Keep a careful eye on them—they can go from golden to charred in a matter of seconds. Transfer to a plate and let them cool completely.

Once the walnuts are cooled, coarsely chop them and tip into a food processor, along with the cashews, garlic, parsley, basil, and oil. Blitz until you have the desired consistency.

Season with salt to taste. If not using immediately, spoon the pesto into a clean jar, cover the top with extra-virgin olive oil, and refrigerate for up to 1 week.

PORK, LEMONGRASS, AND MINT MEATBALLS

½ tablespoon olive oil

2 round shallots, finely diced

1 green chile, halved and seeded

1 lemongrass stalk (white part only), cut into thin slices

1 small handful of mint leaves

1 pound, 2 ounces lean ground pork

1 egg

½ cup panko bread crumbs

Pinch of sea salt and freshly ground black pepper

FOR THE SAUCE

2 tablespoons brown sugar

4 tablespoons water

2 tablespoons soy sauce

2 tablespoons mirin

2 tablespoons lemon juice

1 lemongrass stalk (white part only), cut into very thin slices

Serves 4

These fluffy pork meatballs are served with a light sauce (more of a drizzle), which enhances, rather than detracts from, the peppy Thai flavors of lemongrass and mint. As long as you've got time to chill them in the refrigerator before baking, they make a quick and easy midweek dinner.

Heat the oil in a small skillet over medium heat and fry the shallots for 3 to 4 minutes until softened. Transfer to a plate and let cool.

Put the chile, lemongrass, and mint leaves in a small food processor and whizz until they form a paste. Scrape into a large bowl with the ground pork, cooled shallots, egg, and panko bread crumbs. Season, then mix together with your hands until all the ingredients are well incorporated.

Form 1¾-ounce balls from the mixture by rolling and pressing between your palms—the mixture should make 12 balls. Arrange on a baking sheet lined with baking parchment and chill in the refrigerator for 30 minutes to 1 hour. Preheat the oven to 425 °F.

Bake the chilled meatballs for 16 to 18 minutes, turning the sheet once or twice so all the balls cook evenly, until golden on the outside and cooked through.

Meanwhile, make the sauce by heating the sugar and water in a small pan over medium-high heat. Bring to a boil, then turn down the heat slightly and stir with a wooden spoon until all the sugar has dissolved. Add the soy, mirin, lemon juice, and lemongrass and simmer for 5 minutes until reduced slightly. Strain through a small strainer into a small pitcher (to remove the lemongrass pieces) to drizzle over the meatballs or to serve on the side.

Serve with rice and wilted Asian greens, such as pak choi.

CHEESE-FREE MARGHERITA PIZZA

FOR THE BASE

3½ cups strong white flour,
  ideally "00," plus extra for
  dusting
¼-ounce packet active dry yeast
1¼ cups warm water
1 teaspoon sea salt
1 tablespoon olive oil

FOR THE SAUCE AND TOPPING

14-ounce can good-quality,
  whole tomatoes
½ teaspoon superfine sugar
½ tablespoon extra-virgin
  olive oil
A little olive oil, for frying
4 ounces basil tofu, thinly sliced
  then cut into small pieces
Basil leaves, to sprinkle
Sea salt and freshly ground
  black pepper

Makes 4

Don't tell the purists, but I've added basil tofu to this pizza instead of cheese—lightly fried first to give it a golden deliciousness. To recreate a blisteringly hot pizza oven at home, take a tip from the brilliant Pizza Pilgrims in London: use a skillet. Trust me, it works!

Sift the flour into a large bowl and make a well in the center. Mix the yeast in the warm water until dissolved, then slowly pour into the well, working it into the mixture with a wooden spoon and then, once the mixture starts coming together, with your hands. Add the salt. Bring the dough together into a ball and knead vigorously on a lightly floured counter for 10 to 15 minutes, until nicely elastic. (Hold a portion of dough up to the light and stretch gently—if it tears it needs more kneading, and if it stretches so it is almost translucent, it's ready.)

Grease a large bowl with the oil and add the dough, turning to make sure it is well oiled. Cover with plastic wrap and leave for 1 hour in a warm place until doubled in size. Meanwhile, make the sauce. Put the tomatoes in a pan over medium heat and crush gently with a spoon. Add the sugar and simmer for 10 minutes, until thickened. Stir in the extra-virgin olive oil. Season, then remove from the heat.

Turn the risen dough out onto a floured counter and knock back with the heel of your hand. Divide into 4 balls. Wrap 3 in plastic wrap and set aside in a cool place. Press the remaining dough ball down with your fingertips to create a disk. Place your palms at opposite sides of the disk and gently push them outward to stretch the dough farther, rotating it as you go. (If this is tricky, use a rolling pin, gently.) Once the dough is side-plate-size, pick it up and drape over the knuckles of both hands. Gently pull your hands apart to stretch the dough, rotating it as you go. Do this until it is thin and dinner-plate-size, but thicker around the edges. Repeat with the remaining dough balls.

Heat a little olive oil in a small skillet over medium heat. Fry the tofu for a couple of minutes, until starting to turn golden. Remove from the heat. Preheat the broiler to maximum. Heat a large, heavy-bottom, ovenproof skillet over very high heat. Add a pizza base to the pan, spread a little tomato sauce onto it, leaving a ¾-inch border, and cook for 2 to 3 minutes depending on the strength of your broiler, until the edges start to puff up and the bottom has patches of char. Spread a quarter of the tofu on the sauce, sprinkle with basil, and broil in the pan for 2 to 3 minutes, or until cooked through. Repeat to cook all four pizzas.

LASAGNA

FOR THE RAGU

1 tablespoon olive oil
1 onion, minced
2 garlic cloves, minced
2 stalks of celery, finely sliced
1 pound, 2 ounces ground steak
14-ounce can chopped tomatoes
1 tablespoon tomato paste
½ cup red wine
Small handful of flat-leaf parsley,
　　chopped
Sea salt and freshly ground
　　black pepper

FOR THE BÉCHAMEL SAUCE AND PASTA

2 cups almond milk
1 small onion, minced
1 bay leaf
6 black peppercorns
2 cloves
4 tablespoons dairy-free
　　sunflower spread,
　　plus extra for greasing
⅓ cup all-purpose flour
1 tablespoon mustard powder
¾ cup oat cream
About 9 lasagna sheets (the no-
　　boil kind)
½ teaspoon ground nutmeg
2 tablespoons panko
　　bread crumbs

Deep baking dish, approximately
　　11 x 8½ inches, greased

Serves 6

A lovingly cooked lasagna is a beautiful thing: creamy béchamel, rich ragu, and layers of tender pasta. With this much going on there's no need to smother it in cheese. A dusting of panko crumbs adds a golden crunch to the topping, and a smidgen of mustard powder apes the bite of Parmesan.

For the ragu, heat the oil in a large, heavy-bottom skillet over medium heat. Cook the onion for 5 to 10 minutes until softened. Stir in the garlic and celery and cook for another 3 minutes. Add the ground steak and cook, stirring, for around 4 minutes until browned.

Turn the heat up to medium-high and stir in the chopped tomatoes, tomato paste, wine, and parsley. Season and simmer over low heat, uncovered, for 1 hour.

Meanwhile, make the béchamel. Pour the almond milk into a saucepan and stir in the onion, bay leaf, peppercorns, and cloves. Season with a little salt and bring to a boil, then lower the heat and simmer for 10 minutes (don't worry if the sauce splits a little at this stage) before removing from the heat and letting it infuse until needed. Preheat the oven to 400 °F.

When the ragu is almost ready, melt the dairy-free spread in a separate saucepan over low-medium heat, then add the flour, stirring until you have a smooth roux. Place a strainer above the roux and strain the infused almond milk through it, discarding the onion, bay leaf, and spices (although I like to add some of the onions to the ragu at this stage, rather than wasting them all). Whisk until all the milk is incorporated into the roux, then stir in the mustard powder and simmer for 2 minutes, before adding the oat cream. Simmer for another 2 to 3 minutes, then remove from the heat.

Spread about one-third of the ragu over the bottom of the baking dish and arrange a layer of the lasagna sheets on top, and then a quarter of the béchamel. Repeat until you have three layers of pasta and a thicker layer of béchamel on top.

Sprinkle the nutmeg and panko bread crumbs over the top and bake for around 30 minutes until the top is bubbling and the panko crumbs are golden.

STICKY LIME AND SOY CHICKEN WITH NEW POTATOES, PARSNIPS, AND SHALLOTS

1 ¼ pounds new potatoes, halved
1-2 parsnips, cut into large pieces
2 tablespoons vegetable,
    sunflower, or canola oil, plus
    2 teaspoons for the glaze
2 tablespoons lime marmalade
2 ½ teaspoons soy sauce
1 garlic clove, crushed
6 small round shallots, peeled
    and halved
4 large chicken legs, skin on
Sea salt and freshly ground
    black pepper

Serves 4

This is one of those nifty, one-pan chicken dishes just made for busy nights. Think of it as a mini roast, without the fuss. Sticky lime and soy-glazed chicken legs sit happily roasting on a bed of golden potatoes and parsnips while you get on with your evening, and even the pan juices make a delicious "instant" sauce.

Preheat the oven to 400 °F.

Toss the potatoes and parsnips with the 2 tablespoons of oil. Season, place in a large roasting pan, and roast for 15 minutes.

Mix the lime marmalade, soy sauce, garlic, and the 2 teaspoons of oil together to make a glaze. Add the shallots to the roasting pan, tossing with the potatoes and parsnips. Arrange the chicken legs on top of the vegetables, then brush the tops generously with the sticky lime glaze.

Roast for 50 to 55 minutes or until the chicken is dark gold and the juices run clear, and the vegetables are tender. Serve with green beans and the sauce from the pan.

BEEF SHIN AND CRAFT ALE STEW WITH CRISPY-SAGE DUMPLINGS

FOR THE STEW

2 tablespoons all-purpose flour
1 1/2 pounds beef shin, trimmed and diced
3 tablespoons olive oil
1 onion, diced
2 stalks of celery, trimmed and thickly sliced
2 bay leaves
2 sprigs of thyme
1 1/4 cups beef broth
Scant 1 1/4 cups dark craft ale or porter
3 large carrots, chopped into large chunks
Sea salt and freshly ground black pepper

FOR THE DUMPLINGS

1 teaspoon olive oil
Small handful of fresh sage leaves, finely shredded
2 3/4 ounces suet
1 cup self-rising flour

Serves 4

A classic beef stew to bring comfort on chilly nights. Choose a rich and chocolatey craft ale for the sauce, such as porter, a traditional beer similar to stout. It was named for the river porters in London who used to have it daily with oysters. Porter is having something of a renaissance and is easy to find in grocery stores.

Spread the flour onto a plate and season with salt and pepper. Dredge the diced beef in the seasoned flour to coat.

Heat 2 tablespoons of the oil in a large ovenproof Dutch oven over medium heat. Fry the beef for about 2 minutes on each side, until browned all over, working in several batches so as not to crowd the pan, and adding a little more oil if necessary. Transfer the browned beef to a plate using kitchen tongs or a slotted spoon.

Add the remaining tablespoon of oil to the pan and gently fry the onion for 3 to 4 minutes. Add the celery, bay leaves, and thyme sprigs and cook for another 5 minutes until the vegetables are softened and starting to color. Stir in a little of the broth and deglaze the bottom of the pan. Tip in the rest of the broth, the ale, the beef, and any remaining flour from the plate. Bring to a boil, then turn the heat down, cover, and simmer for 2 hours. Add the carrots, top off with a dash more ale if needed and simmer for another 20 minutes.

Meanwhile, preheat the oven to 350 °F. Heat the oil for the dumplings in a small skillet over medium heat. Fry the shredded sage leaves until crispy, then transfer to a plate lined with paper towels and let cool. Once cool, mince.

Rub the suet into the flour in a bowl with your fingertips until it resembles coarse bread crumbs. Mix in the crispy sage and season with salt. Add just enough cold water, 1 teaspoon at a time, to bring the mixture together into a dough. Roll into small golf-ball-size balls and place on top of the stew (the bottoms should be in the liquid and the top halves exposed). Transfer the Dutch oven to the oven, uncovered, and cook for another 25 to 30 minutes, or until the dumplings are cooked through and golden and crisp on top.

Serve with olive oil mash (see page 85) and collards. A glass of the craft ale wouldn't go amiss either.

PURPLE SPROUTING BROCCOLI WITH LEMON, GARLIC, AND TOASTED ALMONDS

1 tablespoon slivered almonds
7 ounces purple sprouting
   broccoli, ends trimmed
1 tablespoon extra-virgin olive oil
2 garlic cloves, finely sliced
Finely grated zest and juice of
   ½ lemon
Sea salt

Serves 4-6 as a side dish

Purple sprouting broccoli, with its delicate flavor and gorgeous violet florets, is one of the culinary treasures of early spring. It pairs well with strong flavors like garlic, enhanced here by some fresh lemon and a sprinkling of toasted almonds. Delicious with both roasted lamb and chicken.

Toast the slivered almonds in a small, dry skillet over medium-high heat until golden—keep a careful eye on them as they can burn quickly. Remove from the heat and tip onto a plate.

Lightly cook the purple sprouting broccoli in a pan of boiling water for 5 to 6 minutes until just tender, then drain and return to the warm pan.

Meanwhile, heat the oil in a small skillet (use the same one that you toasted the almonds in) over medium-high heat and fry the garlic for 1 to 2 minutes, until it starts to color but not burn. Add the lemon juice and stir.

Pour this mixture over the broccoli and toss to coat. Sprinkle with the toasted almonds, the lemon zest, and a little salt. Serve immediately.

CARAMELIZED CHANTENAY CARROTS

1 pound, 2 ounces Chantenay or
  baby carrots, trimmed
2 teaspoons superfine sugar
1 tablespoon coconut oil
2 tablespoons water
Sea salt and freshly ground
  black pepper
Fresh cilantro, minced,
Sesame seeds, or flat-
  leaf parsley, chopped
  (see recipe)

Serves 4

These sticky, tender baby carrots are a breeze to make and a versatile side dish. To serve with Asian dishes or at barbecues, toss the carrots with sesame seeds and cilantro. To serve with a roast, sprinkle with flat-leaf parsley.

Boil the carrots for 8 to 10 minutes in a large pan of lightly salted water, until just tender. Drain and return to the pan. Turn the heat down to medium and add the sugar, coconut oil, and water.

Stir to coat all the carrots and simmer for 10 to 15 minutes, stirring occasionally, until the carrots are caramelized in patches.

Remove from the heat, season, and toss with either cilantro and sesame seeds or flat-leaf parsley.

DESSERT

COCONUT CUSTARD TARTS

2 tablespoons confectioners'
    sugar
1 pound, 2 ounces block of
    ready-made puff pastry
    (NOT the all-butter kind)
4 egg yolks
2 tablespoons superfine sugar
2 teaspoons cornstarch
1 ¾ cups coconut milk
2 teaspoons vanilla extract
½ teaspoon ground cinnamon

12-section muffin pan, generously
    greased with dairy-free spread

Makes 12

Portuguese custard tarts (*pastéis de nata*) are one of life's greatest little pleasures. But since going dairy-free I've had to stare longingly at them through bakery windows … until I stopped moping and made my own. I've taken a tip from baking guru Richard Bertinet here and dusted the counter with confectioners' sugar—it really gives the pastry a sweet edge.

Lightly dust your counter with the confectioners' sugar and roll out the puff pastry block to a thickness of around ¼ inch. Cut out 12 circles using a 4-inch round cookie cutter. Press these into the sections of the prepared muffin pan. Prick the bottoms of each shell lightly with a fork then put the pan in the refrigerator to chill while you make the coconut custard. Preheat the oven to 400 °F.

Whisk the egg yolks, sugar, and cornstarch together in a bowl. Pour the coconut milk into a saucepan and stir in the vanilla extract. Heat until simmering over low-medium heat, removing it just when it starts to bubble around the edges of the pan; don't let it boil.

Pour onto the egg-and-sugar mixture in a slow, steady stream, whisking constantly with a balloon whisk to combine. Once you've got a smooth custard, return it to the pan and cook over very low heat, stirring with a wooden spoon, until quite thick.

Remove the muffin pan from the refrigerator and pour the custard into the 12 pastry shells. Use a small, fine-mesh strainer to sprinkle a little cinnamon over the tops of the custards. Bake on a high shelf in the oven for 25 minutes, or until the pastry is golden and the custard is set.

Remove from the oven and let cool for 2 minutes in the pan before transferring the tarts to a wire rack to cool. To get the tarts out of the pan, use a dinner knife to go around the edges of each half, then twist to lift up the bottom (and don't worry if a few flakes of pastry fall away or stay behind; it won't impact the tarts' deliciousness). Best eaten when still slightly warm.

RASPBERRY TRIFLE

2 tablespoons sherry
1 tablespoon confectioners' sugar
1 ¾ cups fresh raspberries
Double quantity of whipped
    coconut cream (see page 137)
Toasted, slivered almonds,
    to decorate

FOR THE TRIFLE SPONGES
(Makes around 20)
2 eggs, separated
⅓ cup superfine sugar
½ teaspooon vanilla extract
½ cup all-purpose flour, sifted
Confectioners' sugar, for dusting

FOR THE COCONUT CUSTARD
5 egg yolks
½ cup superfine sugar
2 teaspoons cornstarch
1 ¼ cups coconut milk
Scant 1 cup coconut cream
Seeds of 1 vanilla bean or
    ½ teaspoon vanilla powder
    (optional)
2 teaspoons vanilla extract

Pastry bag, fitted with a plain
    ¾-inch tip, or a disposable
    bag with the end snipped off
    to the right width

Serves 8

Trifle is normally a dairy festival in a glass bowl. Thanks to our trusty friends, coconut milk and cream, you can make this delicious milk-free version (it even won thumbs up from my dad, an ardent trifle fan). Most store-bought trifle sponges contain milk powder, but homemade ones are pretty simple to make. I've adapted the trifle sponges recipe from one for Naples cookies by the food writer Mary-Anne Boermans.

To make the trifle sponges, preheat the oven to 400 °F and grease and line two baking sheets. Whisk the egg whites using an electric whisk, adding half of the sugar a little at a time, and whisk after each addition until you have stiff peaks.

Use the electric whisk to beat the egg yolks, the vanilla extract, and the remaining sugar together, until pale and creamy—this will take about 5 minutes, so keep going until you get the desired consistency. Gently fold the whisked whites into the yolk mixture using a large metal spoon, then gently fold in the flour just until combined. Fill the pastry bag with the mixture, then pipe 2¾-inch-long cookies onto the baking sheet, spacing them well apart. Bake for 10 to 15 minutes until lightly golden and crisp. Let cool, then dust with confectioners' sugar.

Whisk the egg yolks for the custard in a bowl with the sugar and cornstarch. Pour the coconut milk and cream into a saucepan and stir in the vanilla seeds or powder if using, and the vanilla extract. Heat until simmering over low-medium heat, removing it just when it starts to bubble around the edges of the pan; don't let it boil. Pour onto the egg-and-sugar mixture in a slow, steady stream, whisking constantly with a balloon whisk. Once smooth, return it to the pan and cook over very low heat, stirring with a wooden spoon, until it is quite thick—be patient and don't turn the heat up; it **will** thicken. Let cool.

To assemble, arrange the trifle sponges in the bottom of a large glass or trifle bowl so you have a snug layer. You may not need all of them. Pour the sherry on the sponges. In a large bowl, mix the confectioners' sugar and half the raspberries, crushing the berries lightly with a fork to release some of their juices, but still retaining some shape. Layer the crushed raspberries on top of the trifle sponges, then top with the remaining raspberries. Pour the cooled custard over the top and smooth it so you have a flat layer. Refrigerate for 30 minutes.

Remove the trifle from the refrigerator and spoon the whipped coconut cream over the top. Return to the refrigerator for a couple of hours to chill, then sprinkle the toasted, slivered almonds over the top and serve.

ALPHONSO MANGO-AND-LIME PAVLOVA

FOR THE MERINGUE
4 egg whites
Generous 1 cup superfine sugar
2 teaspoons cornstarch
2 teaspoons white wine vinegar
2 teaspoons vanilla extract

FOR THE TOPPING
AND SYRUP
Scant ¼ cup mango juice
Juice of 1 lime and the zest of
    ½ (try to get long strands
    using a zester)
½ cup superfine sugar
1 Alphonso or other ripe mango,
    cut into ¾-inch chunks

FOR THE CREAM
1 ¾ cups coconut cream
1 ½ teaspoons superfine sugar

Serves 6 to 8

Alphonso mangos are the fragrant, buttery King of India's mangos, and the Pav is the Queen of Antipodean puddings. Add a thick layer of whipped coconut cream and a zesty mango-and-lime syrup and you have a dairy-free dessert fit for royalty. If you can't get an Alphonso (which has a short season from April–late May), then choose the ripest, juiciest mango you can. (See photograph on page 106.)

Chill the coconut cream in its carton or can in the refrigerator for at least 4 to 6 hours. Meanwhile, preheat the oven to 275 °F.

Cut out a large piece of parchment paper and draw a circle around a dinner plate on one side. Turn this upside down and place on a baking sheet, greased at the corners so the parchment sticks to the sheet.

Whisk the egg whites with an electric whisk in a large and scrupulously clean metal bowl (use the whisk attachment on your stand mixer, if you have one). Once stiff peaks start to form, add the sugar a spoonful at a time, continuing to whisk until all the sugar is added and incorporated. Add the cornstarch, vinegar, and vanilla and whisk to incorporate. The meringue mixture is ready when it is smooth, glossy, and thick.

Spoon this mixture into the circle on your parchment paper, smoothing with the back of your spoon and adding extra meringue around the edges so it is shallow in the middle and taller around the edge. Make decorative peaks around the edge if you like. Bake for 1 hour, then turn off the oven and let the meringue cool completely, for at least 6 hours or overnight.

Make the syrup by heating the mango juice and lime juice in a saucepan over low-medium heat. Add the sugar and bring to a boil. Boil for 3 minutes or until all the sugar has dissolved, remove from the heat, and let cool.

Take the coconut cream out of the refrigerator and pour away any watery liquid. Whisk with the sugar, using an electric whisk, until thick and fluffy but not too stiff.

Once the meringue has cooled completely, carefully transfer it to a serving plate. Spoon the whipped coconut cream into the shallow center of the meringue to form a thick layer. Arrange the mango on top, drizzle over a little of the cooled mango-and-lime syrup, and sprinkle a little lime zest over the top. Serve with the rest of the mango-and-lime syrup in a pitcher.

AVOCADO CHOCOLATE MOUSSE

3 ripe avocados, peeled and
   pitted
8 ounces semisweet chocolate
1 cup coconut cream
1 tablespoon vanilla extract
2 ½ tablespoons maple syrup

Serves 6

Avocado chocolate mousse is something of a craze on vegan blogs. This is my version, which combines a rich semisweet chocolate and coconut cream ganache with the creamy avocado. I know avocado chocolate mousse sounds weird and vaguely '70s, but it's one of those things you've got to try.

Mash the avocado flesh in a large bowl. Use an electric whisk or the whisk attachment of a stand mixer to whisk the flesh until it is smooth with no lumps.

Chop the semisweet chocolate into very small pieces and place in a large heatproof bowl.

Heat the coconut cream in a small saucepan over medium-high heat. Remove from the heat just before it starts to boil—when you start to see bubbles form around the edges.

Pour the cream over the chocolate and stir gently with a wooden spoon until all the chocolate has melted and you have a smooth ganache. (If there is still a little chocolate that hasn't melted, then fill the empty saucepan with water and bring to a simmer—set the heatproof bowl above the saucepan so it isn't touching the water and melt the last of the chocolate, stirring gently.)

Add the vanilla extract and maple syrup and stir again until combined. Pour this mixture into the bowl with the avocado and whisk for 3 to 4 minutes until the mixture has a fluffy, mousselike consistency. Divide between 6 ramekins and chill for a couple of hours before serving.

RHUBARB AND PRESERVED GINGER CRUMBLE WITH HAZELNUTS

FOR THE FILLING

1 1/4 pounds rhubarb, chopped into 1 1/4-inch pieces

1 1/2 tablespoons diced preserved ginger in syrup

1/2 teaspoon ground cinnamon

1 1/2 tablespoons superfine sugar

2 tablespoons water

1 tablespoon lemon juice

FOR THE TOPPING

7 tablespoons baking margarine (NOT the spreadable kind), plus a little extra for greasing

1 cup all-purpose flour

Scant 1/2 cup superfine sugar

1/2 cup ground hazelnuts

Pinch of sea salt

Serves 4 to 6

At certain times of the year the Call to Crumble (CTC) becomes a loud, nagging voice in my ear. The first is in fall—when all those crisp apples and pears come into season. And the second is in early spring, when bundles of fuchsia-pink rhubarb fill the stores. Try classic rhubarb crumble with a little preserved ginger—it gives it a delicious kick.

Preheat the oven to 350 °F. Grease a deep circular baking dish with a little baking margarine, remove the 7 tablespoons for the topping from the refrigerator, cut into small cubes, and set aside for about 10 minutes.

Toss the rhubarb with the preserved ginger, cinnamon, and sugar. Arrange in the bottom of the baking dish and sprinkle the water and lemon juice on top.

Place the flour, sugar, ground hazelnuts, and salt for the topping in a large bowl. Rub in the diced baking margarine gently with your fingertips just until the mixture resembles unevenly sized bread crumbs. Spoon the crumble topping over the fruit so it is completely covered.

Bake for 40 to 45 minutes, or until the fruit is tender and the topping is golden. Serve with custard or a dollop of whipped coconut cream with vanilla (both on page 137).

APPLE PIE

1 quantity short, sweet crust pie
dough (see page 142)

FOR THE FILLING
Around 1 pound, 2 ounces
cooking apples (about
2 apples), peeled, cored, and
cut into 1 1/4-inch cubes
2 red eating apples, peeled,
cored, and cut into
1 1/4-inch cubes
1/2 cup superfine sugar
1 teaspoon ground cinnamon
1 tablespoon lemon juice
1 tablespoon all-purpose flour
1 egg, beaten
1 tablespoon dairy-free sunflower
spread

9-inch round pie dish

Serves 8

Serve up this golden-topped apple pie to the whole family—no one
will guess it's dairy-free. Just like mom used to make, but with a
sneaky bit of dairy-free spread to help make a delicious, gooey
applesauce inside ...

Make the pie dough following the directions on page 142 and
refrigerate for 30 minutes.

Meanwhile, for the filling, toss the apples with the sugar, cinnamon,
lemon juice, and flour in a large mixing bowl and place to one side.

Place a flat baking sheet on a middle shelf in the oven and preheat
the oven to 375 °F.

Lightly flour your counter, then unwrap the larger ball of chilled
dough and roll out into a 1/8-inch thick circle. Line the pie dish with the
dough, leaving a slight overhang. Brush the inside with a little beaten
egg, then fill with the apple mixture. Dot the dairy-free spread on top
of the apples.

Take the smaller ball of chilled dough and roll out in a circle on the
floured counter until it is 1/8-inch thick. Use your rolling pin to pick up
this circle and lay it over the top of the pie. Press the edges together
with your fingers to crimp and seal. Trim any overhang to leave a neat
edge. Brush the top of the pie with the rest of the beaten egg, then
cut a few steam holes in the top with a paring knife. Bake on top of
the heated baking sheet in the center of the oven for 40 minutes, or
until the top is golden.

Sprinkle with a little sugar, then let rest for 30 minutes before serving.
Serve with custard (see page 137) or ice cream (see page 120), as
desired.

PUMPKIN PIE

FOR THE PIE DOUGH

1½ cups all-purpose flour, plus
    extra for dusting
¼ cup vegetable shortening,
    removed from the refrigerator
    10 minutes before using, diced
¼ cup baking margarine
    (NOT the spreadable kind),
    diced
1 tablespoon sugar
Good pinch of sea salt
1 medium egg yolk
Iced water

FOR THE FILLING

1 15-ounce can pumpkin purée
½ cup + 2 tablespoons superfine
    sugar
½ teaspoon ground cinnamon
½ teaspoon ground nutmeg
½ teaspoon ground ginger
2 large eggs
Scant 1 cup oat cream

9-inch round pie dish
Pie weights

Serves 8

Even the most seasoned pie-eater won't be able to tell that this pumpkin pie, with its flaky crust and creamy filling scented with cinnamon and nutmeg, is made with oat cream. Serve it at your Thanksgiving table and all the dairy-avoiders will be doubly thankful.

Sift the flour into a bowl, lifting the strainer high above the bowl to get more air into your mixture, then add the diced vegetable shortening and baking margarine. Start by using two dinner knives to work the fats into the flour until the mixture is the texture of coarse bread crumbs, then take over with your hands, working quickly and lightly with your fingertips. Work in the sugar, salt, and egg yolk.

Add enough iced water, 1 teaspoon at a time, stirring with the knife to work it in, until the mixture is just moist enough to bring together into a dough with your hands. Gather it into a ball, wrap in plastic wrap, and chill in the refrigerator for 30 minutes. Meanwhile, preheat the oven to 425 °F.

Roll out the chilled dough on a lightly floured counter into a ⅛-inch-thick circle. Line the pie dish with the dough, crimping the edges with your fingertips and leaving a slight overhang. Trim any excess dough and prick the bottom lightly all over with a fork.

Cut out a circle of parchment paper to fit inside the pie. Weigh it down with pie weights, then blind bake for 10 minutes. Remove the pie weights and parchment paper and bake the pie crust for another 5 minutes. Remove from the oven.

Whisk together the pumpkin purée, sugar, and spices in a large bowl. Whisk the eggs and oat cream together in a pitcher, then pour onto the pumpkin mixture and whisk until smooth. Spoon this mixture into the pie crust.

Bake in the oven for 10 minutes, then reduce the oven temperature to 350 °F and bake for another 30 minutes, until the crust is golden and the filling is just set.

Let cool completely in the pan. Serve with whipped coconut cream with vanilla (see page 137).

BREAD-AND-"BUTTER" PUDDING

⅓ cup currants
¼ cup coconut oil, plus extra for
  greasing
6 slices day-old white bread
¼ cup superfine sugar
2 large eggs
2 cups almond milk
½ teaspoon ground nutmeg
1 vanilla bean (or ½ teaspoon
  vanilla powder)

Approx. 10½ x 7-inch baking dish

Serves 4

Bread-and-butter pudding is a traditional British pudding, often made by clever home cooks as a way to use up slightly stale bread. I've adapted my mom's recipe to make a dairy-free b&b (the butter had to go, obviously) with rich, thick coconut oil and a nutmeg-flecked almond milk batter. The result is every bit as carby and comforting (think golden, crisp bread on top and a thick, curranty custard underneath) as the original.

Soak the currants in boiling water for 10 minutes to soften and plump them up a bit. Drain and put to one side.

Warm the coconut oil in a small saucepan over very low heat, just until it is a spreadable consistency. Spread onto each slice of bread and then cut each slice into 4 triangles. Use a little extra oil to grease a medium-size baking dish, about 10½ x 7 inches.

Arrange half of the bread triangles in the bottom of the baking dish. Sprinkle the currants and sprinkle a third of the sugar over the slices. Top this layer with the remaining bread triangles, this time arranged in overlapping rows. Sprinkle with half the remaining sugar.

Beat the eggs and almond milk together and stir in the nutmeg. Split the vanilla bean in half with a sharp knife. Scrape out the seeds and add these to the beaten eggs and almond milk (or add the vanilla powder). Pour this mixture over the bread, leaving the tops of the top layer of bread triangles exposed. Sprinkle the remaining sugar over the top of the bread and let stand for 30 minutes. Meanwhile, preheat the oven to 325 °F.

Bake for 45 minutes or until the custard is set and the bread is golden brown.

POMEGRANATE AND PROSECCO TEACUP JELLIES

4 sheets of sheet gelatin
1 cup pomegranate juice
2 tablespoons superfine sugar
2/3 cup Prosecco, Champagne, or
    other sparkling wine
Handful of very fresh
    pomegranate seeds

TO SERVE (OPTIONAL)
4 teaspoons coconut yogurt
Good handful of coarsely
    chopped pistachios

Makes 4

Who says dairy-eaters get all the best desserts? These jellies are a grown-up reworking of a childhood classic, with delicate and floral pomegranate juice and a hit of Prosecco, which fizzes gently on your tongue.

Soak the gelatin sheets in a bowl of cold water for 5 minutes, until soft.

Heat the pomegranate juice and sugar in a small saucepan over medium heat. Remove the softened gelatin sheets from the bowl, wring out any excess water, and add to the juice and sugar. Stir until dissolved, then remove from the heat. Pour in the Prosecco, stir once just to combine, then set aside to cool.

When the liquid is cool enough to go into the refrigerator, decant into a pitcher and pour into pretty teacups or small glasses. Chill for 1 to 1 1/2 hours, until thickened but not completely set, then remove from the refrigerator and add a sprinkling of pomegranate seeds to each. You may need to stir them in a little. Chill for at least another 3 hours, or overnight.

Serve with a dollop of coconut yogurt and a smattering of chopped pistachios, if you like.

COCONUT MILK ICE CREAM

5 egg yolks
¼ cup + 2 tablespoons
   superfine sugar
2 teaspoons cornstarch
1¼ cups coconut milk
Scant 1 cup coconut cream

FOR VANILLA FLAVOR
Seeds of 1 vanilla bean or
   ½–1 teaspoon vanilla powder
   (optional)
½ teaspoon vanilla extract

**FOR CINNAMON CRUNCH
FLAVOR**
1 tablespoon vanilla extract
½ teaspoon ground cinnamon
1¼ ounces crunchy cinnamon
   cereal flakes (such as
   Cinnamon Toast Crunch),
   coarsely chopped into small
   pieces (check the label to
   make sure it's dairy free)

Ice cream maker

Makes about 20 oz [600 ml]

This ice cream is so luscious and creamy that you'll never hanker after the store-bought stuff again. Once you've mastered the coconut base, you can leave the vanilla out if you want to play up the coconut flavor –to make a coconut and mango ice cream for example. Or you can make the cinnamon crunch variation. It's the contrast between the smooth, creamy base and the buried treasure of the golden nuggets that makes this cinnamon ice cream ridiculously addictive.

Whisk the egg yolks, sugar, and cornstarch together in a bowl.

Pour the coconut milk and cream into a saucepan and stir in the vanilla seeds or powder if using, and the vanilla extract. Heat until simmering over low-medium heat, removing it just when it starts to bubble around the edges of the pan; don't let it boil.

Pour onto the egg yolk-and-sugar mixture in a slow, steady stream, whisking constantly with a balloon whisk to combine. Once you've got a smooth custard, return it to the pan and cook over very low heat, stirring with a wooden spoon, until it is moderately thick–be patient and don't be tempted to turn the heat up; it will thicken eventually. It's thick enough when it can pass the spoon test: when the custard coats the back of your wooden spoon and you run a finger down the back of it, it should leave a clear line. Remove from the heat and let cool.

Once cooled, churn in an ice cream maker according to the directions. Pour into an airtight container and freeze for a couple of hours before serving. Any extra ice cream will store in the freezer for up to 2 weeks.

FOR CINNAMON CRUNCH FLAVOR
Prepare the ice cream as above, adding the vanilla and ground cinnamon with the coconut milk and cream in the saucepan. Continue as instructed until the ice cream has churned in the ice-cream maker. At this stage, when it is a soft-serve consistency, fold in the cinnamon cereal pieces. Freeze as above.

ESPRESSO AND RAW CHOCOLATE GRANITA

1 ¾ cups freshly brewed,
   good-quality espresso,
   piping hot
¼ cup + 2 tablespoons
   superfine sugar
¼ cup cacao nibs

Serves 6

Granita is gelato's ristretto-drinking, all-black-wearing sibling. The dessert—sweet ice crystals typically flavored with lemon, coffee, or orange—is originally from Sicily but there are variations all over Italy. Serve in delicate glasses.

Pour the espresso over the sugar in a large bowl and stir until all the sugar has dissolved. Let cool.

Once cool, pour the mixture into a freezerproof plastic tub or ceramic baking dish—you're looking for something wide and fairly shallow.

Freeze flat on a shelf of your freezer for 2 hours. Use a fork to rake through the mixture—right now it has a Slush Puppie texture but you want to break it up so it forms ice crystals. Return to freezer and repeat this process every half hour—another 3 or 4 times—until the entire mixture has formed into ice crystals.

Remove the mixture from the freezer and use your fork to stir in most of the cacao nibs. Hold some back to sprinkle on top of each serving.

Divide the mixture between small glasses or ramekins and serve immediately.

PANNA COTTA

3 sheets of sheet gelatin
1 ¾ cups almond milk
¼ cup superfine sugar
Seeds from ½ vanilla bean or
    ¼ teaspoon vanilla powder
½ teaspoon vanilla extract

Serves 4

Here's that classic dessert, reinvented without the dairy. Because almond milk is blended with water, these panna cottas are a little delicate. Give them a good 4 to 6 hours to set in the refrigerator and, if you're nervous about turning them out onto plates, serve them in their ramekins.

Soak the gelatin sheets in a bowl of cold water for 5 minutes, or until soft.

Put the almond milk in a saucepan over medium heat. Whisk in the sugar, vanilla seeds or powder, and the vanilla extract. Bring to a simmer, check that all the sugar has dissolved, then remove from the heat.

Remove the softened gelatin leaves from the bowl of water, wring out any excess water, and add to the almond milk mixture, stirring until completely dissolved.

Divide the mixture between 4 small ramekins, greased with just a dab of vegetable oil. Alternatively, you can use espresso cups with round bottoms or dariole molds if you have them. Let cool, then chill in the refrigerator for 4 to 6 hours, or until set but still with a good jiggle.

Remove from the refrigerator. Pour hot water into a shallow baking dish and carefully dunk each ramekin, mold, or cup into the water for a few seconds, then turn out onto a small plate. They should come out easily, but if not then dunk the ramekin in the hot water again or run a very sharp knife (that has been dipped in boiling water) around the inside edge of the ramekin to loosen the panna cotta. Alternatively, serve in the dishes.

Serve with fresh berries or compote.

ROSE AND CARDAMOM RICE PUDDING

Couple of handfuls of unsalted
    pistachios
1 tablespoon coconut oil
½ cup pudding rice
1 ¾ cups coconut milk
Scant 1 cup water
¼ cup superfine sugar
4 cardamom pods, lightly
    crushed with the back
    of a knife
½ teaspoon rose water
Edible rose petals (optional)

*Serves 4 (restaurant-size
portions of this dessert are
rather rich)*

A simple, stovetop rice pudding made with coconut milk, studded with pistachios, and gorgeously fragrant with rose and cardamom. Dairy-free nerd fact: rice pudding is synonymous with dairy now, but did you know that in medieval times it was made with almond milk?

Toast the pistachios in a small, dry skillet over medium heat until golden. Keep a careful eye on them as they can burn quickly. Remove from the heat, transfer to a cutting board to cool, then coarsely chop.

Heat the coconut oil in a large, heavy-bottom saucepan over low-medium heat. Once melted, add the rice and stir to coat. Cook for 1 minute, pour in the coconut milk and water, then stir in the sugar and cardamom pods.

Bring to a boil, then turn the heat down and simmer for 20 minutes, stirring regularly, until the rice grains are tender and plumped up and the liquid has reduced by around half. Pour in a little more water if needed. Remove the cardamom pods, stir in the rose water, and fold in half of the chopped pistachios.

Let cool for 10 minutes, then serve while still warm, decorated with the remaining chopped pistachios and a few edible rose petals, if using. Or let cool completely, chill in the refrigerator, and serve completely cold.

BANANAS FOSTER

3 tablespoons coconut oil
½ teaspoon ground cinnamon
Scant ⅓ cup packed
  brown sugar
4 tablespoons dark rum
4 medium bananas, peeled and
  cut lengthwise into quarters
4 scoops of coconut milk ice
  cream (see page 120)

Serves 4

This kitsch confection of bananas, booze, and ice cream hails from New Orleans. Traditionally the bananas are caramelized with butter, but coconut oil is an ideal alternative—its flavor pairs perfectly with the sticky bananas and rum sauce. It's just begging to be served with a paper umbrella and a couple of hanging cocktail monkeys.

Melt the coconut oil in a large, heavy-bottom skillet over medium heat and, as soon as it's melted, stir in the cinnamon and sugar and cook until all the clumps have gone from the sugar and you have a smooth, thick paste.

Add 1 tablespoon of the rum and stir to combine. Spread the banana quarters out in the pan and fry until sticky and turning golden, turning them over with kitchen tongs halfway through to make sure they are golden all over.

Remove the pan from the heat and gently pour in the remaining rum. Tilt the pan away from you and carefully use a long match or candle lighter to flambé the bananas until the flames die out.

Divide the ice cream between four sundae bowls. Add the banana pieces to each bowl using kitchen tongs, then pour over the rum sauce.

LEMON "CHEESE"CAKE

**FOR THE GRAHAM
CRACKER BASE**

Approximately 20 Graham
  crackers (see page 132, but
  replace the cinnamon with
  2 teaspoons ground ginger,
  and use a plain round or
  square cookie cutter)
½ cup dairy-free sunflower
  spread, melted and cooled

FOR THE TOPPING

Scant 2½ cups vegan cream
  cheese, chilled
1 cup coconut cream, chilled for
  at least 4 hours
1 cup confectioners' sugar, sifted
Finely grated zest and juice of
  2 ½ lemons, plus extra zest,
  finely pared, to serve

8-inch round, springform
  cake pan

Serves 8 to 10

It's cheesecake, Jim, but not as you know it. Take a homemade
Graham cracker base with ground ginger and top with a velvety
layer of vegan cream cheese, whipped into a mousselike texture with
coconut cream and lots of lemon. Delicious.

Coarsely break up 10 ½ ounces of the Graham crackers, then whizz
into fine crumbs in a food processor (or put into a large, sealed
freezer bag and have a good bash with the end of a rolling pin until
you have fine crumbs).

Transfer the crumbs to a large bowl and stir in the melted sunflower
spread. Tip the mixture into the bottom of the cake pan and press
down firmly with a wooden spoon so you have a compact crust with
a smooth top. Chill for 30 minutes.

Meanwhile, to make the topping, whisk together the vegan cream
cheese, chilled coconut cream (drain away any liquid from the can or
carton first), confectioners' sugar, and lemon juice for 3 to 4 minutes,
using an electric mixer or the paddle attachment of a stand mixer,
until fluffy and no clumps of confectioners' sugar remain. Fold in the
lemon zest with a large metal spoon.

Take the cheesecake base out of the refrigerator and spoon the
topping over the top. Smooth the surface with a spatula or palette
knife and return to the refrigerator to chill for at least 4 hours before
serving. To serve, just remove the sides from the pan and sprinkle
lemon zest over the top.

SALTY CARAMEL POPCORN

1 1/2 tablespoons sunflower or
   vegetable oil
Scant 1/2 cup popping corn
Pinch of sea salt

FOR THE CARAMEL
Scant 1/4 cup soft brown sugar
4 tablespoons light corn syrup
2 tablespoons coconut oil
1 teaspoon water
Sea salt

Serves 2 greedy people

It's the age-old dilemma: salty or sweet popcorn? This rich, salted caramel corn is for all those who can't decide. Just add a black-and-white movie, a quilt, and someone to cozy up to for the perfect movie night ...

Heat the oil in a large, heavy-bottom saucepan over medium heat. Pour in the corn and flake in the sea salt. Put the lid on the pan. The corn will start popping after about 1 minute and carry on for another 2 to 3 minutes.

When the popping sounds slow down to longer than 4 or 5 seconds between pops, remove from the heat and let cool slightly in the pan.

Meanwhile, for the caramel, put the sugar, syrup, coconut oil, and water in a saucepan over medium-high heat. Stir constantly with a wooden spoon until the coconut oil has melted and the sugar dissolved. Bring to a boil and let it bubble rapidly for 4 to 5 minutes, stirring constantly, until the mixture is a dark, reddish toffee color.

Tip the popcorn into a large heatproof bowl. Pour the toffee sauce over the popcorn and stir well to coat all the kernels. Let cool slightly and let the toffee sauce harden for around 5 to 10 minutes, then sprinkle with sea salt, stir again, and dig in.

CHOCOLATE TRUFFLES

7 ounces semisweet chocolate
¾ cup coconut cream
1 tablespoon rum
Unsweetened cocoa, finely
    chopped nuts or dry
    unsweetened coconut, to coat

Makes around 20

Sometimes it's the little things that can bother you about living dairy free. Like having to forgo those dainty truffles that come with coffee in posh restaurants, or having to turn down chocolate in the office. So why not make your own truffles? They're really easy—as long as you can cope with a bit of melted chocolate on your kitchen surfaces—and make thoughtful gifts, too. I've made these with rum, but you could try espresso, mint essence, bourbon, orange—have fun experimenting.

Chop the chocolate into very small pieces and place in a large heatproof bowl.

Heat the coconut cream in a small saucepan over medium-high heat. Remove from the heat just as it comes to a boil—as soon as it starts bubbling around the edges.

Pour the cream over the chocolate and stir gently with a wooden spoon until all the chocolate has melted and you have a smooth, thick ganache. (If there is still a little chocolate that hasn't melted, then fill the empty saucepan with water and bring to a simmer—set the bowl above the saucepan so it isn't touching the water and melt the last of the chocolate, stirring gently.)

Stir in the rum and chill in the refrigerator for 4 hours.

Place your chosen coating/s in a dessert bowl/s and line a baking sheet with wax paper.

Remove the truffle mixture from the refrigerator. If you have one, dip a melon baller in very hot water, then use it to scoop out truffle-size balls from the chocolate mixture. Pour a little more hot water over the melon baller between each go. Or use a teaspoon and roll the chocolate between your palms to form a ball (be warned, this gets pretty messy). Roll each truffle in the coating of your choice, then place on the baking sheet. Return to the refrigerator and chill until ready to serve, or to package as gifts.

S'MORES WITH HOMEMADE GRAHAM CRACKERS

FOR THE GRAHAM CRACKERS
1 ¼ cups whole-grain spelt flour
1 ¼ cups all-purpose flour, plus
    extra for dusting
1 teaspoon ground cinnamon
1 teaspoon baking powder
Pinch of sea salt
Scant 1 cup baking
    margarine (NOT the
    spreadable kind), at room
    temperature
Generous ¾ cup packed soft
    brown sugar
1 tablespoon honey
1 egg

FOR THE S'MORES
Semisweet chocolate
Marshmallows

2 baking sheets lined with
    wax paper

Makes about 20 cookies/
10 S'mores

Campfire bananas filled with cheap chocolate were the culinary highlight of my Brownies days. Meanwhile in America, they had it made—Graham crackers crammed with chocolate and a marshmallow all toasty and melty from the campfire. Just add a campfire (or broiler) and your best ghost stories …

Sift the flours, cinnamon, baking powder, and salt together.

Cream the margarine, sugar, and honey together with a wooden spoon until pale and fluffy. Whisk in the egg and 1 tablespoon of the flour. Fold in the rest of the flour mixture with a large wooden spoon until combined. Bring the cookie dough together into a ball, wrap in plastic wrap, and chill for 30 minutes. Meanwhile, preheat the oven to 350 °F.

Lightly dust the counter and rolling pin with flour. Roll out the chilled dough into a rectangle about ⅛ inch thick.

Use a 2½-inch square, fluted cookie cutter to cut out the Graham crackers out. For extra authenticity, use a toothpick or the tines of a fork to make a few rows of evenly spaced holes in the middle of each. Space each cracker well apart on the baking sheets and bake for 12 to 15 minutes, turning the sheets around halfway through cooking time, until nut-brown. Remove from the oven and let cool completely.

To make the S'mores over a campfire, top half of the crackers with a piece of chocolate about the same size as the cracker. Toast the marshmallows on long sticks until golden and gooey. Place a marshmallow on top of the chocolate, place another Graham cracker on top, and press down for a minute to melt the chocolate slightly.

To make indoors, place half the crackers on a lined baking sheet. Top each with a piece of chocolate about the same size as the cracker. Heat the broiler and line another baking sheet with foil. Space out the marshmallows (you need one for each S'more) and broil for about 10 seconds until golden on one top, then carefully turn onto their sides using kitchen tongs and broil. Remove from the heat and place a marshmallow on top of the chocolate, place another Graham cracker on top, and press down for 10 seconds, then leave for a minute to melt the chocolate slightly. Eat immediately.

DISHOOM'S BOMBAY COLADA

FOR THE SYRUP
1 cinnamon stick
1 whole nutmeg
2 cloves
2 cardamom pods
1 vanilla bean
1 1/4 cups sugar
2 1/2-inch piece of ginger, peeled
   and grated
1/2 cup water

Serves 8 to 10

FOR THE COLADA
4 teaspoons chai syrup
   (see above)
1/3 cup coconut cream
1/3 cup pineapple juice
4 teaspoons fresh lime juice
10 cilantro leaves
7 ounces ice cubes
2 tablespoons good-quality rum
   (optional)
Dash of Violette liqueur
   (optional)

Serves 1

TO DECORATE (OPTIONAL)
Pineapple leaf
Candy fennel seeds

Serves 1

Dishoom is an excellent Indian restaurant in London, where the cocktails are as delicious as the daal. I have a mild addiction to their Bombay Colada—a spice-infused take on the guilty-pleasure piña colada (think notes of cardamom and ginger, rather than candied cherries and cocktail umbrellas). This luscious concoction is the brainchild of Carl Brown at Dishoom, who normally makes the Bombay syrup in 5-litre batches. Below is a scaled-down version to make at home, with or without rum.

Make the syrup the night before. Toast the cinnamon stick, nutmeg, and cloves in a small, dry, heavy-bottom skillet over medium heat—just until they start to release their aromas. Keep a careful eye on the pan so they don't burn. Remove from the heat and let cool.

Make a crack in each cardamom pod by scoring with a knife. Split open the vanilla bean with a sharp knife but don't remove the seeds.

Put the sugar in a large bowl and add the cardamom, vanilla, ginger, cinnamon, nutmeg, and cloves. Massage them all into the sugar with your fingertips.

Put the water in a large saucepan and bring to a boil. Once at boiling point, tip in the sugar mixture and keep stirring until all the sugar crystals have dissolved. Remove from the heat and pour into a large pitcher or bowl. Cover and let cool and infuse overnight.

The next day, pour the syrup through a fine-mesh strainer into a pitcher, to strain and remove the spices.

To make a virgin colada, put 4 teaspoons of this syrup, plus the coconut cream, pineapple juice, lime juice, cilantro, and ice in a blender, and whizz until thick and smooth. Pour into a hi-ball glass.

To make an alcoholic version, add the rum to the bottom of the hi-ball glass first, then pour the colada mixture on top, whisking briefly to combine. Discard any extra colada mixture so you have enough room to splash the Violette over the top, if using. Garnish, if you like, with a pineapple leaf and candy fennel seeds. (Store any leftover syrup in an airtight container in the refrigerator for up to 2 weeks.)

ULTIMATE HOT CHOCOLATE

1 cup hazelnut milk
2 ¼ ounces semisweet chocolate, chopped into small pieces
1 ½ teaspoons unsweetened cocoa
½ teaspoon maple syrup
¼ teaspoon vanilla extract or pinch of cinnamon (both optional)
Pinch of salt

Makes 2 cups, or 4 to 6 espresso shots

A rich, giddy-making cup of chocolate, closer in spirit to Montezuma II's goblets of *xocolatl* than those watery brews made with instant chocolate powder. Only the hardiest chocaholic will be able to handle more than a cup ...

Warm 7 tablespoons of the hazelnut milk in a heavy-bottom saucepan over low-medium heat. Add the semisweet chocolate pieces and stir with a wooden spoon until they have melted. Slowly pour in the rest of the hazelnut milk, stirring to combine, then whisk in the cocoa. Turn the heat up to medium, add the maple syrup, vanilla or cinnamon if using, and the salt and bring almost—but not to the boiling point.

Pour into cups or espresso cups and drink immediately.

CHOCOLATE SAUCE

3 1/2 ounces semisweet chocolate
4 tablespoons coconut cream
1 tablespoon dairy-free sunflower
   spread
1/2 tablespoon maple syrup
1/2 teaspoon vanilla extract
Pinch of sea salt

Serves 4

Every cook needs a classic chocolate sauce recipe up their sleeve and this is the dairy-free version (not that your guests need know that, unless you want them to) ...

Bring a pan half-filled with water to a gentle simmer over low-medium heat. Put the chocolate and coconut cream in a heatproof bowl that will sit above—but not touching—the water. Stir until melted, then stir in the dairy-free spread, maple syrup, and vanilla until you have a thick and glossy sauce. If it looks in any danger of splitting, take off the heat and stir.

Stir in the salt, then remove from the heat and let cool for 5 minutes before serving warm.

SALTED CARAMEL SAUCE

4 tablespoons coconut oil
Scant 1/2 cup packed soft
   brown sugar
1/2 teaspoon vanilla extract
1 1/2 tablespoons coconut cream
Pinch of sea salt

Serves 4 (makes around 1 cup)

Salted caramel: two words to make this grown woman go weak at the knees. There's something about the juxtaposition of achingly sweet caramel with a little sea salt that always proves irresistible. Drizzle it over coconut milk ice cream (see page 120) or dark chocolate cake ...

Heat the coconut oil and sugar in a saucepan over medium-high heat, stirring constantly with a wooden spoon until the coconut oil has melted and the sugar dissolved. Stir in the vanilla extract and coconut cream, sprinkle in the sea salt, and simmer for a couple of minutes until you have a smooth and creamy sauce.

CUSTARD

4 egg yolks
1 ½ tablespoons superfine
    sugar
2 teaspoons cornstarch
1 ¾ cups soy or coconut milk
Seeds from 1 vanilla bean or
    ½ teaspoon vanilla powder

Serves 4 to 6

A creamy, luscious custard flecked with vanilla seeds.

Whisk the egg yolks, sugar, and cornstarch together in a bowl.

Pour the soy or coconut milk into a saucepan and stir in the vanilla. Heat until simmering over low-medium heat, removing it just when it starts to bubble around the edges of the pan; don't let it boil.

Pour onto the egg yolk-and-sugar mixture in a slow, steady stream, whisking constantly with a balloon whisk to combine. Once you've got a smooth custard, return it to the pan and cook over very low heat, stirring with a wooden spoon, until it thickens to your desired consistency.

Pour into a pitcher and serve immediately.

WHIPPED COCONUT CREAM

1 cup coconut cream
1 tablespoon superfine sugar
1 teaspoon vanilla extract
    (optional)

Makes 1 cup, or serves
4 to 6 alongside dessert

Whipped coconut cream is an incredibly useful dairy-free topping—and it's delicious. The trick is to leave a carton of coconut cream in the refrigerator as long as possible to thicken up, and to drain away any coconut water before you start to whip it. It doesn't whip up quite as stiff as heavy cream would but it's thick enough to use on desserts, with waffles, and on top of scones and trifles. Use vanilla extract when you want to pair it with traditional desserts, like sponge cakes, and leave it out when you want the coconut flavor to come through, as in the mango and lime pavlova on page 112.

Chill the coconut cream in its carton or can in the refrigerator for at least 4 to 6 hours and preferably overnight.

Take the coconut cream out of the refrigerator and pour away any watery liquid. Whisk the coconut cream and sugar together, and the vanilla extract if using, with an electric mixer until thick and fluffy. Use immediately.

BAKING

BROWNIES

8 ounces semisweet chocolate, 70% cocoa solids
1 1/3 cups packed light brown sugar
Scant 1 cup sunflower oil
1/2 cup unsweetened cocoa
1/2 teaspoon gluten-free baking powder
Pinch of sea salt
1/2 cup ground hazelnuts
3 eggs, lightly beaten

8-inch square pan, greased and lined

Makes 16 squares

"What devilment is this? Witchcraft!" joked my husband when I first told him these brownies were not just dairy but gluten free, too. These gooey, fudgy brownies with a proper crust are made with ground hazelnuts and plenty of 70% semisweet chocolate.
No witchcraft, just good ingredients.

Preheat the oven to 350 °F.

Chop 7 ounces of the chocolate into small chunks. Half-fill a saucepan with water and heat over low-medium heat until simmering. Put the chocolate chunks, sugar, and 7 tablespoons of the oil in a heatproof bowl and place it so it is resting on the rim of the pan, but not touching the water. Stir with a wooden spoon until all the chocolate has melted. Remove from the heat and set aside to cool a little.

Meanwhile, chop the remaining 1 ounce of chocolate into chocolate-chip-size chunks and set aside. Sift the cocoa, baking powder, and salt together in a separate bowl and stir in the ground hazelnuts.

Using an electric whisk, or the paddle attachment of a stand mixer, gradually add the beaten eggs, 2 tablespoons of the cocoa mixture, and the remaining oil to the melted chocolate mixture until they are all combined and you have a glossy mixture.

Fold in the remaining cocoa mixture with a large metal spoon just until combined. Stir in the chocolate chip pieces.

Spoon the mixture into the prepared pan, smooth the surface, and bake for 25 to 30 minutes until the top has formed a crust and the inside is cooked but still fudgy. Let cool for at least an hour in the pan before cutting into squares.

BASIC PIE DOUGH

FOR SWEET BASIC PIE DOUGH

Scant 2¼ cups all-purpose flour

5 tablespoons vegetable shortening, removed from the refrigerator 10 minutes before using, diced

5 tablespoons baking margarine (NOT the spreadable kind), chilled and diced

2 tablespoons superfine sugar

1 egg yolk

Pinch of salt

Iced water

Makes 1 pound, 2 ounces, enough to line and top a 9-inch pie

Make everything from blueberry pies to pastries with this versatile basic pie dough. There are two variations—a sweet crust to use in dishes like the apple pie on page 115, and a savory crust that you can make with lard for great flavor, or baking margarine if you're vegetarian. Vegetable shortening is very hard when removed from the refrigerator, so taking it out 10 minutes before you start making the dough ensures it's still cold but just softened enough to work with.

Sift the flour into a mixing bowl (lift the strainer high above the bowl to get more air into your mixture), then add the diced vegetable shortening and baking margarine. Start by using two dinner knives to work the shortening into the flour until it is the texture of coarse bread crumbs, then take over with your hands, working quickly and lightly with your fingertips. Work in the sugar, egg yolk, and salt.

Add the iced water, a teaspoon at a time, and stir with the knife to work into the mixture. Only continue to add it until the mixture is just moist enough to bring together with your hands to form a dough. Gather it into a ball, wrap in plastic wrap, and refrigerate for 30 minutes before using.

FOR SAVORY PIE DOUGH

Scant 2¼ cups all-purpose flour

Pinch of salt

5 tablespoons vegetable shortening, removed from the refrigerator 10 minutes before using, diced

5 tablespoons lard, chilled and diced (or you can use baking margarine to make the pastry vegetarian or vegan)

Iced water

Makes 1 pound, 2 ounces, enough to line and top a 9-inch pie

Make as above, but omit the egg yolk and sugar, and add the salt with the flour.

LEMON CURD

4 eggs, plus 2 egg yolks
2 teaspoons cornstarch
7 tablespoons dairy-free
  sunflower spread
Grated zest of 2 lemons, plus the
  juice of 3
Scant 1 cup superfine sugar
Pinch of sea salt

Makes 1 jar

A truly voluptuous lemon curd to spread on toast, in a Victoria
sandwich, or in the show-stopping lemon meringue sponge on
page 156 ...

Beat the whole eggs, yolks, and cornstarch together in a large bowl
and set aside.

Put the dairy-free spread in a saucepan over medium heat, stirring
until it starts to melt.

Add the lemon zest, juice, sugar, and salt. Keep stirring constantly
until the spread has all melted and the sugar has dissolved. Strain
through a strainer into another pan or large bowl and return the
strained liquid to the pan over low-medium heat.

Pour in the beaten egg mixture in a slow, steady stream, whisking
constantly to combine. Keep whisking until the mixture has the
consistency of thick custard.

Remove from the heat. Let cool completely, then pour into a sterilized
jar and seal. Store in the refrigerator and use within 1 week.

A PROPER AFTERNOON TEA

1. SCONES

Scant 1 ⅔ cups self-rising flour,
   plus extra for dusting
1 teaspoon baking powder
½ teaspoon sea salt
¼ cup baking margarine
   (NOT the spreadable
   kind), removed from the
   refrigerator 15 minutes before
   using, diced
2 tablespoons superfine sugar
½ cup almond or soy milk,
   plus extra for brushing

TO SERVE
Jam
1 quantity whipped coconut
   cream with vanilla
   (see page 137)

Makes 6 large scones

No afternoon tea would be complete without freshly baked scones, still warm from the oven. Slather them with jam and top with a dollop of whipped coconut cream. A big pot of tea is, of course, mandatory.

Preheat the oven to 425 °F and grease a baking sheet.

Sift the flour, baking powder, and salt into a bowl. Lightly rub the baking margarine into the flour with your fingertips (make sure you have cold hands for this bit), just until the mixture resembles large bread crumbs. Mix in the sugar with your fingertips.

Pour in the almond or soy milk a little at a time (you may not need all of it) and bring the mixture together into a dough.

Lightly flour the counter and roll out the dough gently with a rolling pin (don't press down too hard) to a thickness of ¾ inch. Cut out the scones using a round 2½-inch cutter.

Brush the tops of the scones with a little almond or soy milk. Space out on the prepared baking sheet and bake for 10 to 12 minutes until well risen and golden. Let cool on a wire rack.

Serve with a layer of jam topped by a dollop of the whipped coconut cream (or the other way around, if so inclined).

2. EGG AND CHIVE FINGER SANDWICHES

2 eggs
1 tablespoon good-quality
    mayonnaise (check the label to
    make sure it's dairy free)
Small handful of chives, minced
4 thin slices soft white bread,
    crusts removed
Sea salt and freshly ground
    black pepper

Makes 8

These dainty sandwiches are a must at any proper afternoon tea. Arrange them in neat, Jenga-style stacks on your tea stand.

Hard-boil the eggs, then let cool for 10 minutes before peeling. Coarsely chop into small pieces with a fork in a mixing bowl. Stir in the mayonnaise and then the chives. Season and then spread onto half the slices of bread. Top with the other slices, cut into neat rectangles, and serve immediately.

3. SMOKED SALMON FINGER SANDWICHES

2 large slices smoked salmon
Lemon juice
4 thin slices soft white bread,
    crusts removed
Freshly ground black pepper

Makes 8

Keep smoked salmon sandwiches dairy-free by omitting the butter or spread. After all, they're going to be eaten immediately and no one wants the aftertaste of margarine spoiling all that beautiful salmon.

Trim any rough edges off the smoked salmon and cut into smaller slices if needed. Squeeze a little lemon juice on the salmon and grind a little black pepper on top.

Place the slices of smoked salmon onto two of the slices of bread. Place the other slices of bread on top and cut into neat rectangles. Serve immediately.

4. VICTORIA SANDWICH

1 cup canola oil
Generous 1 cup superfine sugar
4 medium eggs
1 ⅔ cups self-rising flour, sifted
1 tablespoon vanilla extract
Confectioners' sugar, for dusting

FOR THE FILLING
1 cup coconut cream
1 teaspoon vanilla extract
1 tablespoon superfine sugar
Fresh strawberries OR
    raspberry jam

2 x 8-inch round cake pans,
    greased and lined

Serves 10 to 12

The Victoria sandwich is the cornerstone of British baking—a simple sponge, spread with cream or buttercream, and sandwiched together with jam. It's just too good to live without on a dairy-free diet. Luckily, this golden sponge, sandwiched with pillowy whipped coconut cream and fresh strawberries (or jam, if you prefer), is every bit as delicious as a classic Victoria sandwich—and I've tried it out on lots of committed butter-eaters!

Chill the coconut cream for the filling in its carton or can in the refrigerator for at least 4 to 6 hours and preferably overnight.

Preheat the oven to 350 °F.

Beat the oil and sugar together using an electric whisk or the paddle attachment of a stand mixer for a few minutes, until well combined.

Add the eggs one at a time, alternating with a tablespoon of the flour each time and whisking to combine. Whisk in the vanilla and fold in the remaining flour, using a large metal spoon, until just combined.

Spoon the cake batter into the prepared pans. Smooth the tops, then bake on the middle shelf of the oven for 20 to 25 minutes, or until the tops are golden and a skewer or toothpick inserted into the middles comes out clean.

Let cool for 5 minutes in the pans, before turning out onto a wire rack to cool completely.

Meanwhile, take the coconut cream out of the refrigerator and pour away any watery liquid. Whisk with the vanilla and sugar, using a handheld electric whisk or whisk attachment of a stand mixer, until thick and fluffy. Return the cream to the refrigerator until the cake is completely cool.

Slice the strawberries, if using, and arrange on the surface of the cake you want to go on the bottom, or spread raspberry jam over the surface. Spoon coconut cream onto the other cake, leaving a small border around the edge of the cake (you probably won't need all the cream). Sandwich the two together gently, sift a little confectioners' sugar over the top of the cake and serve.

BLACK AND WHITE COOKIES

Scant 1 cup superfine sugar
½ cup dairy-free sunflower
   spread
2 ¼ cups all-purpose flour
Scant ¼ cup cornstarch
½ teaspoon baking powder
Pinch of salt
2 eggs
½ teaspoon vanilla extract
¾ cup almond milk
Grated zest of ½ lemon

FOR THE FROSTING

2 cups confectioners' sugar
1 cup dairy-free sunflower spread
Approx. ½ teaspoon vanilla
   extract
4 ½ tablespoons unsweetened
   cocoa

Makes 10 large cookies

Black and white cookies are as New York as the Empire State Building and vulgar taxi drivers. They even cameo'd in a Seinfeld plot. You'll find them shrink-wrapped on the counter of every deli and bodega in the city, but those fondant-smothered versions are rarely a patch on those made in family-run bakeries. I much prefer them with frosting and stippled with lemon zest, the way they serve them at Glaser's Bake Shop, a 100-year-old bakery on the Upper East Side.

Preheat the oven to 375 °F. Grease and line two baking sheets.

Cream together the sugar and dairy-free spread with a wooden spoon in a large bowl, until pale and fluffy.

Sift the flour, cornstarch, baking powder, and salt together in a separate bowl. Add one of the eggs, the vanilla extract, and 1 tablespoon of the flour mixture to the creamed sugar mixture and beat with an electric whisk, or paddle attachment of a stand mixer, until combined. Whisk in the second egg and the almond milk.

Fold the remaining flour mixture into the batter with a large metal spoon, then fold in the lemon zest.

Using an ice-cream scoop, place a scoop of cookie dough on one of the prepared baking sheets and flatten down gently into a circle with the back of the scoop. Repeat with the remaining dough, so you have 5 on each tray, spacing the cookies well apart. Bake for 15 to 20 minutes until golden, then let cool on the baking sheets for 5 minutes, before turning out onto a wire rack to cool completely. (These have a cakey texture, not a crumbly one.)

When the cookies are completely cool, make the frosting. Cream together the confectioners' sugar and dairy-free spread with an electric whisk or paddle attachment of a stand mixer until creamy and smooth, with no lumps (this will take a few minutes). Transfer half to a separate bowl and stir in the vanilla extract. Whisk the cocoa into the other half.

Place a piece of wax paper with a straight edge halfway across each cookie. Use a small spatula or palette knife to smooth the chocolate frosting onto one half of all the cookies. Repeat with a clean spatula, frosting all the other halves with the vanilla frosting.

SHORTBREAD

1 ¼ cups baking margarine
(NOT the spreadable kind),
at room temperature, diced
⅔ cup superfine sugar,
plus extra for sprinkling
½ teaspoon vanilla extract
2 cups all-purpose flour, sifted
1 ¼ cups rice flour, sifted
Good pinch of sea salt

10½ x 7½-inch baking pan,
greased and lined

Makes 20 slices

Make a big pot of tea and help yourself to a slice or three of this crisp and crumbly shortbread.

Beat the baking margarine, sugar, and vanilla together in a large bowl, using a wooden spoon, until pale and fluffy.

Sift together the flours and salt and add to the creamed mixture. Fold together using a large metal spoon and then bring together with your hands into a smooth dough.

Place the dough in the prepared pan and press down lightly with your palm or the back of a wooden spoon to make a smooth, flat layer. Chill in the refrigerator for 30 minutes. Meanwhile, preheat the oven to 325 °F.

Bake for 40 minutes or until lightly golden. Remove from the oven, sprinkle with a little sugar, and score about 20 slices with a sharp knife. Let cool completely in the pan before cutting the slices with the sharp knife. Store any leftover shortbread in an airtight container—it will keep for a few days.

CHOCOLATE BIRTHDAY CAKE

1 ¼ cups self-rising flour, sifted
½ cup unsweetened cocoa
1 teaspoon baking powder
Pinch of salt
1 cup canola or vegetable oil
Generous 1 cup superfine sugar
4 medium eggs

FOR THE GANACHE
10½ ounces semisweet
  chocolate, finely chopped
Generous 1¾ cups coconut
  cream, room temperature
2 tablespoons confectioners'
  sugar, sifted
5 tablespoons coconut cream,
  chilled

TO DECORATE
Multicolored sprinkles

2 x 8-inch round cake/sandwich
  pans, greased and lined

Serves 6 to 8

This is everything a good chocolate cake should be: a light and moist sponge, creamy chocolate filling, and a rich, glossy ganache frosting. And sprinkles—everybody loves sprinkles. (See photograph on page 138.)

Preheat the oven to 350 °F. Sift the self-rising flour, cocoa, baking powder, and salt together in a large mixing bowl. Beat the oil and sugar together with an electric whisk, or with the paddle attachment of a stand mixer, for a few minutes until well combined. Add the eggs one at a time, alternating with a tablespoon of the flour-and-cocoa mixture, and whisk to combine. Fold in the rest of the flour using a large metal spoon, until just combined.

Divide the cake batter between the two pans. Smooth the tops, then bake on the middle shelf of the preheated oven for 20 to 25 minutes, or until the tops are golden brown and a skewer or toothpick inserted into the middles comes out clean. Let cool for 5 minutes in the pans before turning out onto a wire rack to cool completely.

Once the cakes have cooled, make the ganache. Heat the coconut cream in a saucepan over medium-high heat. Remove from the heat just as it comes to a boil—as soon as it starts bubbling around the edges. Put the chocolate pieces in a heatproof bowl, pour the coconut cream over, and stir gently with a wooden spoon until all the chocolate has melted and you have a smooth, thick ganache. (If there is still a little chocolate that hasn't melted, then fill the empty pan with water, bring to a simmer, and set the bowl above the pan so it isn't touching the water, to melt the last of the chocolate, stirring gently.) Whisk in the confectioners' sugar. Transfer 8 tablespoons of ganache to a separate, smaller bowl. Chill both bowls for 10 minutes.

Remove the smaller bowl of ganache from the refrigerator. Add the chilled 5 tablespoons of coconut cream (pour away any remaining watery liquid) and whisk with an electric mixer/paddle attachment of a stand mixer until it is a pale, milk-chocolate shade and mousse-y in texture, with the consistency of heavy cream. Spread over the center of one of the cakes, leaving a ½-inch gap around the edge of the cake. Place the other cake on the top. Remove the remaining ganache from the refrigerator and spread over the top of the cake, letting it spill over the sides. Use a palette knife or spatula to smooth the sides to give you your base coat of frosting. Spread on a second layer to cover any patches where you can still see the sponge, and smooth again. The cake should now be covered with ganache, with no sponge visible. Decorate with sprinkles. Set for 5 to 10 minutes before serving.

CRANBERRY, CHERRY, AND BOURBON MINCE PIES

FOR THE MINCEMEAT
Generous ½ cup dried
  cranberries
3½ ounces dried cherries
4 ounces vegetarian suet,
  shredded
1 cooking apple, skin on, cored
  and cut into ½-inch cubes
  (about 8½ ounces in total)
½ cup packed dark brown sugar
1 cup slivered almonds, coarsely
  chopped
14 ounces dried mixed fruit
Finely grated zest and juice of
  2 oranges
½ teaspoon ground ginger
½ teaspoon ground allspice
1 teaspoon ground mixed spice
½ teaspoon ground cinnamon
5 tablespoons Bourbon

FOR THE PIE DOUGH
1¾ cups all-purpose flour, plus
  extra for dusting
Pinch of salt
Finely grated zest of 1 orange
½ cup vegetable shortening,
  removed from the refrigerator
  10 minutes before using, diced
Iced water
Confectioners' sugar, for dusting

About 3 sterilized jars
2 12-section muffin trays, lightly
  greased with dairy-free spread

Makes 24

Mince pies are the Marmite of Christmas foods—people either love them or hate them. I'm convinced the latter camp have been put off by sickly, soggy, store-bought pies. These light little bakes—with a rich and juicy cranberry and cherry filling and short, flaky dough—have converted many a naysayer.

Combine all the mincemeat ingredients, except for the Bourbon, in a large Dutch oven and stir to combine. Cover and leave overnight.

The next day, preheat the oven to 250 °F. Remove the lid, cover the top of the Dutch oven with foil, and bake for 3 hours. Let cool completely before stirring in the Bourbon. Spoon into the sterilized jars and leave for a minimum of 1 to 2 weeks before making your mince pies. Any mincemeat you don't use in the pies will keep for next Christmas if you store it in a cool, dark place.

To make the pies, sift the flour and salt into a bowl, lifting the strainer high above the bowl to get more air into the mixture. Stir in the orange zest, then add the diced vegetable shortening. Start by using two dinner knives to work the shortening into the flour until it is the texture of coarse bread crumbs (you may find you need to use your hands after a while and, if so, make sure they are cold). Add enough iced water, a very little bit at a time and stirring it in with the knife, for the mixture to be just moist enough to bring together with your hands into a dough (you may not need it all). Gather it into a ball, wrap in plastic wrap, and chill for 30 minutes.

Place two flat baking sheets in the oven and preheat to 425 °F. Take the chilled dough out of the refrigerator and roll it out on a lightly floured counter to a ¹⁄₁₆ inch thickness (it should be very thin). Cut out 24 circles with a 2¾-inch round cookie cutter and press into each section of the trays. Pull the trimmings together into a ball and return briefly to the refrigerator while you fill each pastry shell with 1 teaspoon mincemeat.

Roll the remaining dough out to ¹⁄₁₆ inch thickness and use a small star cutter to cut out 24 star-shape lids. Place these on top of the mincemeat; the points of the stars should touch the edge of the pie shell. Transfer the trays to the preheated trays in the oven and bake for 10 to 12 minutes, until the tops are golden. Remove and let cool slightly on a wire rack before dusting with confectioners' sugar.

JAMMY DOUGHNUTS

7 tablespoons almond milk

1½ cups strong white bread flour

¼-ounce packet active dry yeast

Good pinch of sea salt

2 teaspoons superfine sugar, plus extra to dust

1 egg

2 tablespoons dairy-free sunflower spread, melted and cooled

Sunflower or vegetable oil, for deep-frying

Seedless jam—strawberry, raspberry, or blueberry

Deep-fat fryer

Pastry bag fitted with a thin tip

Makes 8 medium or 10 smaller doughnuts

The doughnut may have taken a recent turn in the spotlight (I'm looking at you, Cronut), but while all those headline-grabbing experiments and novelty flavors are fun, you can't beat a warm jammy doughnut dusted in sugar. They always remind me of standing against the wind on Brighton Pier, eating hot doughnuts from a paper bag while fending off seagulls.

Heat the almond milk in a small pan or in a microwave until lukewarm. Cover and set aside.

Sift the flour into a large mixing bowl. Mix in the yeast, salt, and sugar, then make a well in the center.

Whisk together the egg, warmed almond milk, and melted spread, then pour into the well. Bring together into a large ball of dough. Transfer the dough to a lightly oiled counter and knead for about 10 minutes, until smooth and bouncy (you can also do this with the dough hook attachment on a stand mixer if you don't fancy the upper-arm workout).

Place the dough in a lightly oiled, large bowl, cover with plastic wrap, and leave in a warm place for about 1 hour, until doubled in size.

Divide the risen dough into 8 to 10 evenly sized pieces. Shape each piece into a ball, first by tucking all the edges underneath, then by rolling with your hands into a smooth ball. Place all the balls, well spaced apart, on a lined baking sheet. Cover with a clean dish towel and let rise in a warm place for 45 minutes to 1 hour—they should be nearly doubled in size.

Heat the oil in a deep fat fryer to 375 °F and deep-fry the doughnuts in batches. Alternatively, heat the oil (carefully) to 375 °F in a large, heavy-bottom skillet. The doughnuts are ready when they are golden brown all over. Remove to a plate lined with paper towels. Sprinkle superfine sugar onto a separate plate and roll the hot doughnuts in it. Transfer to a wire rack and let cool for 10 minutes.

Use the tip of the pastry bag tip or a skewer to make a hole in one side of each doughnut. Fill the pastry bag two-thirds full with jam, then pipe a little into each hole. Serve warm.

HORCHATA WITH OATMEAL COOKIES

FOR THE HORCHATA

½ cup long-grain white rice

1 ⅓ cups blanched almonds

1 cinnamon stick (Mexican if you can find it)

2 ½ tablespoons maple syrup

1 tablespoon vanilla extract

Pinch of sea salt

4 cups cold, filtered water

A little ground cinnamon, to sprinkle (optional)

FOR THE COOKIES

½ cup raisins

½ cup dairy-free sunflower spread

¾ cup packed soft brown sugar

½ cup all-purpose flour

½ teaspoon baking powder

½ teaspoon ground cinnamon

Pinch of sea salt

1 medium egg

1 teaspoon vanilla extract

2 cups rolled oats

Makes about 3½ cups horchata and 10 to 12 medium cookies

Here is the dairy-free answer to milk and cookies. Horchata originates from Valencia, where it's made with tiger nuts (*chufa*), which are tricky to find outside of Spain. You can drink it there in old-fashioned *horchaterías* lined with pretty tiles. Horchata traveled with the Spanish to Latin America and there are regional versions all over that continent. Mexican horchata is one of the best known and is usually made with rice and cinnamon. Almonds are often used too, and help make the milk really creamy. It makes the perfect partner to chewy oatmeal cookies, fragranced with cinnamon.

For the horchata, put the rice, almonds, and cinnamon stick in a bowl. Cover with double the volume of cold water, cover, and let soak for 8 hours or overnight.

For the cookies, soak the raisins in boiling water for 5 minutes. Drain then pat dry with paper towels. Grease and line two baking sheets. Cream together the dairy-free spread and sugar, using a wooden spoon, until pale and fluffy. Sift the flour, baking powder, cinnamon, and salt together in a separate bowl. Add the egg, vanilla, and 1 tablespoon of the flour mixture to the sugar and dairy-free spread mixture and beat with an electric whisk, or paddle attachment of a stand mixer, until combined. Fold in the remaining flour mixture using a large metal spoon, then fold in the raisins and oats. Form the dough into a ball, wrap in plastic wrap, and chill in the refrigerator for 30 minutes. Meanwhile, preheat the oven to 350 °F.

Use an ice cream scoop to scoop out cookie-size balls of the chilled dough. Space these out well apart on the prepared baking sheets (5–6 per sheet) and flatten down slightly with a spoon. Bake for 10 to 12 minutes, or until golden around the edges but still soft-ish in the middle. Remove from the oven and let cool for 5 minutes, then transfer to a wire rack to cool completely.

Meanwhile, for the horchata, rinse and drain the rice, almonds, and cinnamon. Chop the cinnamon stick into smaller pieces and add with the rice, almonds, maple syrup, vanilla, and salt to a blender. Pour in the filtered water and blitz until the almonds, cinnamon, and rice are broken up into very small pieces and you have a creamy liquid (this will take a few minutes). Place a fine-mesh strainer over a large bowl and line with cheesecloth. Pour the horchata mixture into the strainer, using a wooden spoon to press down and push more liquid through. Add ice to hi-ball glasses and pour over the horchata. Serve with a little sprinkling of ground cinnamon on top, if desired, and the cookies.

SOUR CHERRY AND ALMOND FLAPJACKS

1 tablespoon coconut oil

²/₃ cup dairy-free sunflower
spread

¼ cup light corn syrup

¾ cup packed soft brown sugar

3 ½ cups rolled oats (look for
gluten-free oats if you want
to make them gluten free)

2¾ ounces dried regular or sour
cherries

Scant ½ cup toasted, slivered
almonds

10 ½ x 7 ½-inch rectangular
baking pan, greased and lined

Makes 12

Banish the butter and make traditional flapjacks with dairy-free spread to bind and a little coconut oil for taste—its subtle flavor masks the spread and pairs well with the tang of dried cherries (sweet or sour) and toasty almonds.

Preheat the oven to 375 °F.

Melt the coconut oil and dairy-free spread with the syrup and sugar over low heat, stirring with a wooden spoon until all the ingredients have melted and are combined. Stir until a dark golden color, then stir in the oats, dried cherries, and slivered almonds.

Spread the mixture into the prepared pan. Cover any cherries poking out of the top with oats to prevent them from burning in the oven, and press the top down firmly with the back of a wooden spoon.

Bake for 25 to 30 minutes until starting to turn golden.

Remove from the oven and let cool in the pan for 5 minutes before scoring 12 squares with a sharp knife. Let cool completely in the pan before cutting into squares. Store in an airtight container for a few days.

PHILIPPA'S LEMON MERINGUE CAKE

1 cup dairy-free sunflower spread
1 ¼ cups superfine sugar
4 medium eggs
1 ½ cups self-rising flour, sifted
Grated zest of 2 lemons (long
   strands are preferable) and
   1 tablespoon juice
2 tablespoons soy or almond
   milk
¾ cup ground almonds
1 ½ teaspoons baking powder

FOR THE FILLING AND TOP
4 egg whites
1 ½ cups superfine sugar
1 quantity lemon curd
   (see page 143)

8-inch round, deep cake pan
   greased and lined with
   wax paper
Pastry bag, fitted with a
   plain tip
Kitchen blowtorch

Serves 8 to 10

My friend Philippa is an amazing baker and creates beautiful, towering wedding cakes and birthday confections in her spare time. For my bachelorette, my friends surprised me with a dairy-free afternoon tea, and Philippa's three-tiered lemon cake with toasted peaks of meringue was the spectacular centerpiece ...

Preheat the oven to 350 °F.

Using an electric whisk, or the paddle attachment of a stand mixer, beat the dairy-free spread with the sugar until pale and fluffy. Whisk in the eggs, one at a time, alternating each with 1 tablespoon of the flour and whisking to combine. Mix in the lemon zest, juice, and soy or almond milk. Fold in the remaining sifted flour, the ground almonds, and baking powder using a large metal spoon.

Spoon the batter into the prepared pan and bake for 1 hour to 1 hour and 15 minutes. To test whether the cake is cooked all the way through, pop a wooden stick (kebab stick is perfect!) into the center and push all the way down. If it is sticky when removed, then the cake will need more time, and if a few crumbs stick to the sides then the cake is ready to come out.

Leave the cake in the pan for 5 minutes, then remove from the pan and transfer to a wire rack to cool completely. When the cake is completely cool, cut horizontally into equal thirds using a bread knife (rounded tip is best) or a cake leveler.

For the filling, put the egg whites and sugar in a bowl set over a pan of simmering water and whisk on high speed, using a handheld electric whisk, for 5 to 10 minutes until the mixture is thick and glossy with stiff peaks.

Place one layer of the sponge on a plate or cake stand, spread with lemon curd, then a layer of the soft meringue. Place another layer of sponge on top, and repeat.

Add the final layer of sponge and, using a pastry bag, pipe small whirls on the soft meringue over the top until it is fully covered. Alternatively, you can use a palette knife to spread a layer of meringue on the top and create little peaks for texture. Using a kitchen blowtorch, lightly flame the peaks so that they color on top.

PASSION FRUIT FRIANDS

5 egg whites
2 cups confectioners' sugar, plus
    extra for dusting (optional)
1 1/4 cups ground almonds
1/2 cup all-purpose flour, sifted
Generous 3/4 cup dairy-free
    sunflower spread, melted
    and cooled
1/2 teaspoon vanilla extract
Pulp of 2 passion fruits

12-section friand or cupcake pan,
    well greased with dairy-free
    spread

Makes 12

Walk into any good café in Sydney or Melbourne and you'll see a rack of friands on the counter. These airy cakes get their name from the French word *friandise*—meaning dainty or confection. The delicate vanilla sponge is studded with sharp passion fruit, a combination that proves irresistible to everyone who crosses its path.

Preheat the oven to 400 °F.

Whisk the egg whites in a very clean bowl, using an electric mixer, for a couple of minutes until white and frothy.

Sift the confectioners' sugar onto the egg whites. Add the ground almonds, sifted flour, melted spread, vanilla, and passion fruit pulp. Use a large metal spoon to gently fold everything into the egg whites, trying not to knock out too much air.

Divide the batter equally between the sections of the greased friand tray. Bake for 20 minutes in the preheated oven, or until golden around the edges and lightly golden on top, and a small skewer or toothpick inserted into the center of one comes out clean.

Let cool for 5 minutes in the pan, before turning out onto a wire rack to cool further (use a dinner knife to help get them out of the pan—go around the edges and then lift out with the knife). Dust with a little confectioners' sugar if you like.

LEMON AND ROSEMARY OLIVE OIL CAKE

Finely grated zest of 3 lemons
4-5 teaspoons fresh rosemary
    needles, minced
    (depending on how
    pronounced you want the
    rosemary flavor to be)
Generous 1 cup superfine sugar
1 cup olive oil
4 eggs
1 ⅔ cups self-rising flour, sifted
Pinch of salt

FOR THE DRIZZLE TOPPING
Juice of 1 ½ lemons
Scant ¼ cup water
Scant ½ cup superfine sugar
Zest of ½ lemon (try to get
    long strands using a zester),
    to decorate

2-pound loaf pan, greased
    and lined

Serves 8 to 10

This is a cross between a classic British lemon drizzle cake and a sultry, Mediterranean olive oil cake. The fresh lemon zest and hint of rosemary make me think of shaded Italian squares, hiking in Cypriot pine forests, and late nights fueled by limoncello—even when eating a slice on a rainy day, accompanied by nothing stronger than a big mug of tea.

Preheat the oven to 350 °F.

Rub half of the lemon zest and the rosemary into the sugar with your fingers. Beat the olive oil and sugar together with an electric whisk or with the paddle attachment of a stand mixer for a couple of minutes.

Add the eggs one at a time, alternating with a tablespoon of the flour, and whisk to combine. Fold in the remaining flour using a large metal spoon, until just combined. Fold in the other half of the lemon zest, and the salt.

Pour the mixture into the loaf pan and bake for 45 to 50 minutes, or until the top is golden and a skewer or toothpick inserted into the middle comes out clean.

Remove the cake from the oven and let cool for 5 to 10 minutes in the pan before turning out onto a wire rack with a sheet of foil spread underneath it. Prick small holes all over the top of the cake with a fork or a skewer.

While the cake is cooling, make the drizzle topping. Heat the lemon juice in a pan along with the water. Add the sugar and bring to a boil, stirring occasionally. Boil for 3 minutes or until all the sugar has dissolved and the mixture has a runny, syrupy consistency, then remove from the heat and let cool slightly.

While the cake is still warm, pour half of the syrup all over the top of the cake and let it sink in before pouring over the other half, allowing some to drip down the sides. Decorate with lemon zest.

STRAWBERRY AND ELDERFLOWER MILLEFEUILLE

1 cup coconut cream
1 tablespoon confectioners'
    sugar, plus extra for sprinkling
1 pound, 2 ounces ready-made
    puff pastry (NOT the all-butter
    kind)
1 ½ tablespoons elderflower
    cordial
1 ½ cups ripe strawberries,
    trimmed and thinly sliced
    (about ⅙ inch),
    plus extra, whole, to serve
Fresh elderflower heads,
    to decorate (optional)

Makes 6

Millefeuille is a classic French confection—tiers of pastry and cream that translates as "a thousand leaves." Meanwhile, the combination of strawberries and heady elderflowers is as English as Wimbledon and country garden parties. Think of this as an Anglo-French alliance in pastry form.

Chill the coconut cream in its carton or can in the refrigerator for at least 4 to 6 hours and preferably overnight.

Preheat the oven to 400 °F and place a large baking sheet in to heat. Grease and line a second large baking sheet.

Flour the counter with the confectioners' sugar. Roll out the pastry into a large rectangle, about 12 x 10 ½ inches and ⅛-inch thick. Trim the edges, using a ruler to ensure a straight line.

Drape the pastry over a rolling pin and carefully unfurl onto the lined baking sheet. Prick the pastry all over lightly with a fork and sprinkle with a little more confectioners' sugar. Place the preheated baking sheet on top to weigh down the pastry, then place a heavy Dutch oven on top of this to really weigh it down. Transfer to the oven and bake for 25 minutes or until the pastry is golden. Remove from the oven and let cool.

When the pastry is cool, and with a long side facing you, use a sharp knife and a ruler to cut the pastry into 3 evenly sized rows across and 6 evenly sized rows down, to give 18 rectangles of the same size.

To make elderflower cream, take the coconut cream out of the refrigerator and pour away any watery liquid. Whisk with the elderflower cordial using a handheld electric whisk until thick and fluffy, for 3 to 4 minutes.

To assemble a millefeuille, spoon some elderflower cream onto a pastry rectangle. Lay strawberry slices flat on top, then top with another pastry rectangle. Repeat, then top with a final pastry rectangle, so that each millefeuille has 3 layers of pastry. Use a small, fine-mesh strainer to dust the top with confectioners' sugar. Smooth the edges using the edge of a palette knife so the cream and pastry form neat sides. Repeat to make 6 millefeuille in total. Serve with extra strawberries on the side and decorate with fresh elderflowers, if you can find them.

NEAPOLITAN ICED BUNS

Scant 1 cup almond milk
3 ½ cups strong white bread
  flour, plus extra for dusting
¼-ounce packet active dry yeast
Generous pinch of sea salt
¼ cup superfine sugar
2 eggs
3 oz [85 ml] water

FOR THE ICING
2 ⅔ cups confectioners' sugar
1-2 tablespoons boiling water
½ teaspoon vanilla extract
½ tablespoon unsweetened
  cocoa
½ teaspoon strawberry
  flavoring
¼ teaspoon pink food coloring

Makes 12

While my childhood snacking policy could be summarized as Chocolate First, there were other sweet treats that caught my fancy. Iced buns–those long, soft subs topped with a thick slick of icing were one. Neapolitan ice cream, evenly portioned into a flag of strawberry, vanilla, and (of course) chocolate ice cream, was another. Iced buns have a bread roll base, so are naturally dairy-free; Neapolitan ice cream is obviously not. So I've combined these two retro favorites into one. Presenting ... Neapolitan iced buns.

Heat the almond milk in a small pan or in the microwave until lukewarm. Cover and set aside.

Sift the flour into a large bowl. Mix in the yeast, salt, and sugar then make a well in the center. Whisk together the eggs, warmed almond milk, and water, then pour into the well. Bring together into a ball of dough, knead lightly for a couple of minutes in the bowl, then transfer to a floured counter and knead for 10 minutes, until smooth and bouncy. (You can also use the dough hook attachment on a stand mixer, if you don't fancy the upper-arm workout.) Transfer the dough to a lightly oiled bowl. Cover with plastic wrap and leave in a warm place for about 1 hour, until doubled in size.

Divide the dough into 12 evenly sized pieces. Shape each piece into a ball, first by tucking all the edges underneath, then by rolling with your hands into a smooth ball. Roll out each ball into a sausage shape, or "finger," about 3 inches long. Line a large baking sheet with parchment paper, then arrange the 12 dough fingers, evenly spaced, on the sheet. Cover with a dish towel and let rise in a warm place for 45 minutes–they should be nearly doubled in size. Meanwhile, preheat the oven to 400 °F.

Bake the risen buns for 12 minutes or until golden, then transfer to a wire rack to cool completely. Once cool, make the icing. Sift the confectioners' sugar into a bowl and whisk in enough boiling water to make a smooth, stiff paste. Divide into three bowls. Whisk vanilla extract into one and cocoa into another (plus a little extra water if needed to loosen just slightly). Whisk the strawberry flavoring into the third bowl of icing. Check to taste before adding the pink food coloring a drop at a time, just until you get a pastel pink shade.

Dip 4 of the buns into the vanilla icing, 4 into the chocolate icing, and 4 into the strawberry icing. Let the icing set, then eat.

FAIRY CAKES

7 tablespoons dairy-free sunflower spread
½ cup superfine sugar
2 large eggs
¾ cup self-rising flour
1 teaspoon vanilla extract

FOR THE ICING
1 ⅓ cups confectioners' sugar
1 tablespoon boiling water
Sprinkles or sugar stars to decorate (always check the label to make sure they don't contain milk powder)

12-section cupcake tray, lined with mini-cupcake liners

Makes 12

Fairy cakes are the cupcake's smaller, less showy sister. These dainty, old-fashioned bakes are topped with a pond of glacé icing and a smattering of sprinkles. My dairy-free version is the perfect cake recipe for children: they're easy to make together (as long as you don't mind confectioners' sugar EVERYWHERE), and you can take them along to a birthday party or fête and make another dairy-free kid's day.

Preheat the oven to 350 °F.

Cream the sunflower spread and sugar together in a large bowl using an electric whisk or the paddle attachment on a stand mixer until the mixture is very pale and fluffy and all the sugar is incorporated, about 2 to 3 minutes.

Add one of the eggs and half the flour to the mixture and beat again until incorporated. Add the remaining egg, the remaining flour, and the vanilla, and beat again.

Divide the mixture evenly between the liners and bake for 20 to 25 minutes in the preheated oven until the tops are golden and a toothpick inserted into the center of one of the cakes comes out clean. Turn the cakes out onto a wire rack and let cool.

To make the glacé icing, sift the confectioners' sugar into a bowl and add the boiling water. Mix to a thick, smooth paste, then spread over each cake using the back of a teaspoon. Sprinkle each cake immediately with decorations and let the icing set before eating.

RAINY-DAY CARROT CAKES

½ cup golden raisins
½ cup sunflower, vegetable, or
  canola oil
Scant 1 cup packed soft brown
  sugar
¾ cup self-rising flour
¾ cup whole-grain spelt flour
1 teaspoon baking powder
½ teaspoon baking soda
Pinch of salt
2 teaspoons ground cinnamon
1 teaspoon ground mixed spice
½ cup walnuts, chopped into
  very small pieces
2 eggs
7 ounces carrots, peeled and
  coarsely grated

FOR THE FROSTING
1 ½ lemons (for zesting) and
  2 teaspoons juice
1 cup vegan cream cheese
1 ⅓ cups confectioners' sugar,
  sifted
Pinch of salt

10 ½ x 7½-inch rectangular
  cake pan, greased and lined

*Makes 12 large squares or
24 small ones*

It's raining, it's pouring, and the sky is the color of a wet seal—what you need is a square of carrot cake topped with zesty lemon frosting. Hopefully you'll have everything you need to make the cake in your pantry already, though sourcing the vegan cream cheese might take a little forethought (it's widely available from health food stores and many supermarkets).

Soak the golden raisins in a little boiling water for 5 minutes to plump them up. Drain and pat dry with paper towels. Preheat the oven to 325 °F.

Beat the oil and sugar together using an electric whisk or with the paddle attachment of a stand mixer, for a couple of minutes.

Sift the flours, baking powder, baking soda, salt, cinnamon, and mixed spice into a large bowl. Use 1-2 tablespoons of this flour mixture to lightly coat the walnut pieces and golden raisins, in a separate bowl (to help prevent them from sinking in the cake).

Add the eggs to the oil-and-sugar mixture, one at a time, alternating each with a tablespoon of the flour mixture and whisking to combine.

Fold in the remaining flour mixture using a large metal spoon, until combined. Fold in the carrots and then the walnuts and golden raisins.

Spoon the batter into the prepared cake pan and smooth the top. Bake for 35 minutes, or until a skewer or toothpick inserted into the middle comes out clean. Let cool in the pan for 5 minutes, then transfer to a wire rack to cool completely.

For the frosting, finely grate 1 tablespoon of lemon zest. Whisk the vegan cream cheese, confectioners' sugar, lemon zest, and juice together, using an electric whisk or the paddle attachment of a stand mixer, for 3 to 4 minutes until fluffy and any clumps of confectioners' sugar have disappeared. Refrigerate until the cake is completely cool.

Once the cake is completely cool, spread the frosting on the top of the cake, right to the edges, smoothing the top and edges with a palette knife. Cut into squares. Use a lemon zester to zest long strands of the remaining lemon zest and use to decorate each square.

RASPBERRY AND
DARK CHOCOLATE MUFFINS

7 tablespoons dairy-free
   sunflower spread
Scant 1 cup whole-grain spelt
   flour
Scant 1 cup all-purpose flour
1 teaspoon baking soda
2 teaspoons baking powder
½ cup superfine sugar
4 ¾ ounces semisweet
   chocolate, chopped into very
   small chunks
1 ¼ cups raspberries
2 eggs, beaten
⅔ cup vegetable oil
1 tablespoon granulated sugar,
   to sprinkle

12-section muffin tray, lined with
   muffin liners

Makes 12

Store-bought muffins don't hold a candle to homemade, especially the "free-from" ones with all those unpronounceable ingredients. These muffins are a breeze to make, and are crammed with sharp raspberries and chunks of semisweet chocolate.

Melt the dairy-free spread in a small saucepan over low heat and let cool completely. Preheat the oven to 400 °F.

Sift both flours into a large mixing bowl. Add the baking soda and baking powder and fold together gently using a large metal spoon. Gently fold in the sugar, chocolate chunks, and raspberries, still using the large metal spoon.

Add the beaten eggs, oil, and the cooled, melted spread. Stir just until all the ingredients are combined—don't overmix. The raspberries will break up as you fold.

Fill each muffin liner almost to the top (using an ice-cream scoop helps get the same amount into each liner) and sprinkle the tops with a little granulated sugar. Bake for 15 to 20 minutes or until golden.

Cool on a wire rack. The muffins taste best when still slightly warm, while the chocolate is still melted and cozy inside.

DARK CHOCOLATE
AND PEAR BANANA BREAD

3 medium, or 2 large, very ripe
bananas (about 14 ounces)
²⁄₃ cup baking margarine
(NOT the spreadable kind),
at room temperature
¾ cup packed soft brown sugar
1 cup all-purpose flour
1 cup whole-grain spelt flour
2 teaspoons baking powder
½ teaspoon baking soda
3 teaspoons ground ginger
Pinch of salt
1 ¾ ounces dried pears, cut into
¼-inch cubes
2 medium eggs
Scant ½ cup canola or
vegetable oil
2 ¾ ounces semisweet
chocolate, chopped into very
small pieces

2-pound loaf pan, greased
and lined

Makes 1 loaf

A throw-together banana bread fragranced with a little ginger and
with nuggets of melted semisweet chocolate and juicy pear hidden
inside ...

Preheat the oven to 350 °F.

Mash the bananas with a fork. In a separate bowl, cream the baking
margarine and sugar together with an electric whisk or with the
paddle attachment of a stand mixer until pale and fluffy. Stir in the
bananas with a large metal spoon.

Sift the flours, baking powder, baking soda, ground ginger,
and salt together in another bowl. Toss the diced pear pieces in
2 tablespoons of the flour mixture and set aside.

Add the eggs to the creamed sugar and banana mixture one at a time,
alternating with a tablespoon of the flour mixture and beating after
each addition. Fold in the rest of the flour mixture with a large metal
spoon, until just combined. Next, stir in the oil until just combined,
then fold in the semisweet chocolate and pear pieces.

Spoon the batter into the loaf pan and smooth the top. Bake in the
preheated oven for 45 to 50 minutes or until the top is dark golden
and a skewer or toothpick inserted into the middle comes out clean.

Let cool in the pan for 5 minutes before turning out onto a wire rack.
Let cool completely before slicing.

GINGERBREAD GENTLEMEN

Scant 1¼ cups all-purpose flour,
  plus extra for dusting
3 teaspoons ground ginger
½ teaspoon ground mixed spice
1 teaspoon ground cinnamon
Pinch of salt
1 teaspoon baking soda
½ cup baking margarine
  (NOT the spreadable kind), at
  room temperature, cut
  into small cubes
½ cup packed soft brown sugar
1 egg
3 tablespoons light corn syrup

TO DECORATE
Black icing writing pen
White icing writing pen

Gingerbread man cutter

*Makes 16 to 20 depending on the
size of your cutter*

Meet the gingerbread gentlemen: aristocrats with jaunty iced bow ties and monocles. These Bertie Wooster cookies make for a thoughtful gift, packaged in clear cellophane bags and tied with a ribbon. Best accompanied with a large pot of Earl Grey tea … and a butler.

Sift the flour, spices, salt, and baking soda together in a large bowl.

Beat the margarine and sugar together with an electric whisk or the paddle attachment of a stand mixer until pale and fluffy. Add the egg and 1 tablespoon of the flour mixture and whisk briefly to combine, then whisk in the syrup. Fold in the remaining flour using a large metal spoon to combine and bring it together with your hands into a ball of dough. Wrap in plastic wrap and chill in the refrigerator for 30 minutes. Meanwhile, preheat the oven to 325 °F. Grease and line two baking sheets.

Lightly flour a counter and roll the dough out with a rolling pin to a thickness of about ⅙ inch. Cut out cookies using a gingerbread-man cutter and space them out on the prepared baking sheets—8-10 on each sheet.

Bake for 15 minutes or until golden. Let the cookies cool for 5 minutes on the baking sheets, then transfer to a wire rack to cool completely.

Once cool, use the white icing pen to draw on details such as a shirt collar, buttons, mouth, and eyes. Use the black icing writing pen to draw irises in the eyes, a monocle around one eye, and a bow tie (use the white icing pen if you want your gentlemen to be sporting white ties).

DAIRY-FREE DIRECTORY

I've tried, wherever possible, to use ingredients that are easy to track down in your local grocery store or health food store. Here's where to track down some harder-to-find items, along with brand recommendations and websites.

ALMOND MILK

Almond milk is now widely available. You'll increasingly find it available in cafés, too. There are lots of brands on the market. I think unsweetened tastes fresher and more pleasant, and is always my preferred choice for cooking. Look for brands made with non-GMO ingredients. Some are also fortified with vitamins and additional calcium. I like Almond Breeze (made by Blue Diamond).

www.bluediamondalmonds.com

BASIL TOFU

Try Taifu basil tofu, which is available from some health food stores in Europe and online.

www.taifun-tofu.de/en

CACAO NIBS

Most health food stores will now stock cacao nibs. Brace yourself for the price as they are not cheap (around $8 for an 8-ounce bag), but a little will go a very long way. They can be found in health food stores, as well as online.

www.navitasnaturals.com

UNSWEETENED COCOA

Unsweetened cocoa is available in all major grocery stores, but check the label to make sure it doesn't contain milk in the ingredients. I like Green & Blacks Organic Cocoa, which should be fine if you have a lactose intolerance, as it doesn't contain any dairy ingredients. However, like most cocoas it does have a 'may contain milk' disclaimer because of the factory where it is produced. Cocoa produced in a milk-free factory can be tricky to find. If you have a milk-protein allergy, try organic fair trade unsweetened cocoa from Lake Champlain.

us.greenandblacks.com
www.lakechamplainchocolates.com

COCONUT CREAM AND MILK

There are dozens of brands of coconut milk. For whipped coconut cream I get the best results from chilling a carton of coconut cream. Please note that it's coconut cream you're after, rather than creamed coconut (which is sold in solid blocks).

www.sodeliciousdairyfree.com

COCONUT OIL

You should now find coconut oil stocked in the same grocery store aisle as olive and sunflower. There are several decent options on the market including Gold Label Virgin Coconut Oil from Tropical Traditions and organic coconut oil from Wilderness Family Naturals, which can be found online.

www.tropicaltraditions.com
www.wildernessfamilynaturals.com

COCONUT YOGURT

CoYo is a great coconut yogurt brand available in health food stores and online. It makes both small and medium tubs of its plain yogurt. Coconut yogurt can also be bought online from So Delicious Dairy Free.

www.coyo.com
www.sodelciousdairyfree.com

DAIRY-FREE SUNFLOWER SPREAD

Dairy-free, vegan sunflower spread can be bought online from Vegan Essentials.

www.veganessentials.com

SEMISWEET CHOCOLATE

Seventy percent cocoa-solids dark chocolate is widely available. As with cocoa, semisweet chocolate sometimes comes with a 'may contain milk traces' warning if it was made in a factory that also handles milk products. If you have a milk protein allergy, make sure it's vegan chocolate.

www.veganessentials.com

OAT CREAM

Oatly produces cartons of oat cream that are stocked in some in health stores in Europe and Asia. (It's called 'Organic Creamy Oat' and has a similar consistency to light cream.)

www.oatly.com

PANKO

Increasingly available in supermarkets, from Japanese and Asian grocery stores and from online retailers. Most brands I've tried, including Saitaku, have been pretty good.

www.saitaku-food.com/en
www.kikkomanusa.com

SOYA YOGURT

I use plain Alpro Soya Yogurt.

www.alpro.com/

VANILLA POWDER

A little pot of vanilla powder goes a long way, helps make those dairy-free bakes taste delicious, and takes away the fuss of scraping vanilla seeds from a bean. You can find it in health food stores and online.

www.vivapura.com

VEGAN CREAM CHEESE

You can source vegan cream cheese in independent health food stores and online.

www.kite-hill.com

For more help, recommendations, and tips on going dairy free, visit my website:
dairyfreedelicious.com

INDEX

ACKNOWLEDGMENTS

Although this book has my name on the cover, it wouldn't have happened without the support and creativity of some very talented and generous people.

First, thanks to everyone at Quadrille. Thanks for making this book look even better than I'd dared hope. Huge thanks to Jane O'Shea for believing in the idea and understanding that it should be joyful and beautiful, not preachy or dull. I'm indebted to Céline Hughes for her advice and thoughtful editing. Thanks to Helen Lewis and Katherine Keeble for the gorgeous design. And thanks to publicity whiz Ed Griffiths and the sales team.

To my agent Tim Bates—thanks for believing in me and in this project, and for all those Notes coffees.

Laura Edwards—thanks for your gorgeous photos. You are such a talent and I'm so glad you shot this book. Tabitha Hawkins—no one in the world does props better than you.

Thanks to the lovely Emily Jonzen for your super styling and perfection with a citrus zester, ably assisted by Poppy Campbell and Camilla Baynham. Ladies, you all made the shoot such a blast.

Thanks to the editors who encourage me and commission me—particularly Susan Smillie at *The Guardian* and Sarah Randell and Helena Lang at *Sainsbury's Magazine*. Plus William Sitwell, to whom I owe a huge amount.

Thanks to Sarah Tye at Gemma Bell PR and Carl Brown at Dishoom for the Bombay Colada recipe.

Huge love to my family for their help in testing (and enthusiastically eating) all those bakes: Jo and Trevor Salter, Ed, Jess, and Finley Salter. Sorry if your freezers are still full of cake. Plus, a big thanks to my first-rate recipe testers and supportive friends, Ellie Porter, Vanessa Brooks, and Elaine Brooks. Philippa Tuck is a baking queen—thank you Flips for your amazing lemon meringue sponge recipe. Thanks to Lucia Rae, Adrienne Pitts, and Sukhpal Sahota for encouragement and for that Sunday-afternoon shoot when this book was still very much an idea.

Finally, thanks to Jon Yeomans, my no. 1 cheer-person, clearing-up-in-chief, proof-reader, and consumer of countless recipe tests. I couldn't have done it without you.